Bible and Mission

Christian Witness in a Postmodern World

Bible and Mission

Christian Witness in a Postmodern World

Richard Bauckham

Easneye Lectures
Frumentius Lectures

A Division of Baker Book House Co

First published jointly in 2003 by Paternoster Press in the UK
and Baker Book House in the USA

Reprinted 2005

11 10 09 08 07 06 05   8 7 6 5 4 3 2

Paternoster Press is an imprint of Authentic Media,
9 Holdom Avenue, Bletchley, Milton Keynes, MK1 1QR, UK
www.authenticmedia.co.uk/paternoster

Baker Academic is an imprint of Baker Book House Company,
PO Box 6287, Grand Rapids, MI 49516-6287
www.bakeracademic.com

British Library Cataloguing in Publication Data
A catalogue record for this book is available from the British Library

ISBN 1-84227-242-X

Library of Congress Data
Library of Congress Cataloging-in-Publication Data is on file
at the Library of Congress, Washington, D.C.
ISBN 0-8010-2771-3

Unless otherwise stated, Scripture quotations are taken from the
New Revised Standard Version Bible, copyright 1989,
Division of Christian Education of the National Council of the Churches of Christ
in the United States of America. Used by permission. All rights reserved.

Cover Design by FourNineZero
Typeset by WestKey Ltd, Falmouth, Cornwall
Printed and bound in Denmark by Nørhaven Paperback, Viborg.

Contents

The Easneye Lectures

Easneye is the name of a small hill on the edge of the River Lea, twenty-five miles north of London, between the town of Ware and the village of Stanstead Abbotts in Hertfordshire, England. It was purchased in 1867 by the son of Sir Thomas Fowell Buxton, 'The Liberator', who had been responsible, with William Wilberforce, for the abolition of the slave trade.

Since 1971 Easneye has been the home of All Nations Christian College, which since its foundation in 1923 has been training people for intercultural Christian mission – people who continue to come from all over the world and to go to the ends of the earth for the sake of the gospel.

Lady Hannah Buxton, widow of Sir Thomas, in a letter written to her grandson on 8 May 1869, expressed this prayer for the fine building at Easneye:

> That it may ever be inhabited by faithful servants of God in and through Christ Jesus, and that it may ever be a habitation of God in the hearts of the inhabitants by the Holy Spirit, and Christ be honoured, confessed and served, and this place be a fountain of blessing in the church and in the world.

This vision constantly inspires those who live, work and study at All Nations, and the Easneye Lectures are prepared and published in the same spirit. The lectures are delivered as an annual series at All Nations by a visiting guest lecturer who is noted in the field of missiology. The purpose of the lectures is to enhance the level of theological reflection on the practice of mission, to explore the riches of mission history throughout the world and to contribute to current debates surrounding missiological issues and challenges.

*   *   *   *   *

This series of Easneye Lectures was first delivered by Professor Richard Bauckham at All Nations Christian College in the autumn of 2001. Subsequently, in the spring of 2002, he delivered the same lectures in Ethiopia at the Ethiopian Graduate School of Theology in Addis Ababa, under the title Frumentius Lectures.

For the majority of Christians mission starts and ends with Matthew 28:18–20. This text occupies a significant place in our understanding of mission, but is just the apex of everything the Bible has to say about God and mission.

Professor Bauckham, undoubtedly one of the church's leading thinkers, has in this volume given us the benefit of his rich explanation of the theme of mission in the Bible.

The advance of the church throughout the world has suffered somewhat, not only from decline in numbers attending, particularly in western countries, but also in a lack of confidence in the propriety of leading others to Christ throughout the world. Many Christians are struggling with an identity crisis. Are we really meant to go out and make disciples of all nations?

What attracts me to the contents of this volume in particular is the manner in which Professor Bauckham presents a thoroughgoing understanding of mission from God's perspective. This is not something dependent on one or two isolated verses, but is systematic and consistent exploration of the theme throughout the Scriptures. This volume is destined to stimulate Christians' thinking and to encourage those who feel a lack of confidence in the whole mission enterprise.

I warmly commend the book to practitioners of mission, to teachers of mission, to students of mission, to all Christians involved in the mission of the world.

Joe M. Kapolyo
Principal
All Nations Christian College

The Frumentius Lectures

It requires but a short time in a country like Ethiopia to see that poverty in the developing world extends well beyond economic deprivation. In some ways want of money is but a symptom. More fundamental is the poverty of resources, education, and access to ideas, information and opportunities to engage in conversation about the things that matter most. The isolation these poverties produce impoverishes us all.

It was partly these concerns that led to the establishment of the Frumentius Lectures by the Ethiopian Graduate School of Theology in 1999. The lectures were named after the Syrian missionary who brought the gospel to the remote Ethiopian highlands in the fourth century. The subsequent 1600 years of Christian history in Ethiopia are a very rich legacy, but one largely isolated from the rest of the Christian world.

The Frumentius Lectures given by Professor Bauckham and presented in revised form in this volume were a marvellous stimulus for taking the gospel in Ethiopia beyond Ethiopia. Not only did the lectures provide penetrating biblical and theological reflection on the nature of Christian mission in today's world, but Professor Bauckham's warm engagement with Ethiopian Christians and genuine interest in the development and state of Christianity in Ethiopia provided a wonderful example of what it means to be a world Christian. We are very grateful.

Steve Bryan
Ethiopian Graduate School of Theology
Addis Ababa

Author's Preface

The seed from which this book grew was a lecture on 'Mission as Hermeneutic for Scriptural Interpretation', which I gave in Cambridge in November 1999. It was part of a series of lectures on Mission in Theology, sponsored by the Currents in World Christianity Project, and I am grateful to Dr Brian Stanley, director of the project, and to Professor Daniel Hardy, convenor of the lecture series, for inviting me to give the lecture and thereby stimulating me to think about mission in a very broadly biblical way.

As a result of that lecture Dr Christopher Wright, who was then Principal of All Nations Christian College, invited me to give a series of the annual Easneye Lectures at All Nations College on this theme. I am grateful to him for inviting me and so challenging me to fill out the sketch I had presented in Cambridge into a more detailed and developed exploration of the theme. Then Dr Steve Bryan of the Ethiopian Graduate School of Theology invited me to give the Frumentius Lectures in Addis Ababa, and it seemed to me that the same lectures would be appropriate for both audiences.

By the time I gave the Easneye Lectures in the autumn of 2001 Joe Kapolyo had succeeded Chris Wright as Principal. I am grateful to him and to others (especially Richard Harvey and Richard Briggs) who made me welcome and discussed the lectures with me. It was a privilege to contribute something to the life of a community dedicated to the church's mission worldwide.

My Frumentius Lectures in Addis Ababa, given in February 2002, were the third series of these annual public lectures sponsored by the Ethiopian Graduate School of Theology. It was an honour to give lectures named after the man who brought the Christian gospel to Ethiopia in the fourth century. My time in Ethiopia was a wonderful experience of discovering that this country, economically one of the very poorest in the world, is so very rich in Christian history and tradition, art and culture, and in living and active Christian faith today. I suspect that Addis Ababa, with its eight theological colleges (Ethiopian Orthodox, Protestant [Kaleheyeet and Mekane Yesus], Mennonite, Pentecostal and Roman Catholic) and its many gifted and committed theological students, will increasingly play a role as a centre of theology and mission, not only for the growing churches of Ethiopia but also further afield.

There are many people who helped to make my time in Ethiopia a rewarding experience. I should like to thank especially Steve and Dawn Bryan, Mistru Kebede, Debela Birri, Paul and Lila Balisky, Bill and Stephanie Black, Erik and Kim Redelfs, Art and Sue Volkmann, Simeon Mulatu, Phil Johnson, Bill and Sarah Goodman, Ivar Vegge, Tony Weedor and Yosef Bezeded.

In Lalibela in northern Ethiopia I learned the legend of the building of the extraordinary churches that were carved out of the solid rock in the twelfth century. King Lalibela employed a huge workforce that laboured during the hours of daylight, but during the hours of darkness the angels worked, and to the amount of stonecutting achieved by the human labourers added twice as much. This seemed to me a parable of the way that God can make of what we do in his service much more than we can make of it ourselves. I have written this book with that thought in mind.

Richard Bauckham
St Andrews, March 2003

Chapter 1

A Hermeneutic for the Kingdom of God

1. The World after 9/11 – between McWorld and Jihad?

A major theme of this book is going to be the relationship between the particular and the universal. In the later months of the year 2001 immense newspaper space was given to reflection on the events of 11 September 2001, or 9/11 as Americans call it, and what they tell us about the world as we must all now recognize and live in it. As a starting point for this book, I am selecting one such comment, because it raises the question of the particular and the universal in a way that will pose issues we must grapple with in the rest of the book.

The British newspaper *The Times* has a regular column of religious comment on current affairs. On 3 November 2001 this Credo column was written by Jonathan Sacks, the Chief Rabbi of Britain. With the horror of 11 September very much in mind, Jonathan Sacks' article was a plea for diversity and particularity against what he calls 'universalist cultures'. These are cultures that consider they possess universal truth and therefore set out to convert the world to this truth or (and he implies this is likely to be the result) to impose it forcibly on the world. This cultural universalism is 'the cultural counterpart of imperialism'. In the past, western civilization has known five such universalist cultures: Ancient Greece, Ancient Rome, medieval Christianity, Islam and the Enlightenment civilization of western modernity and its influence. All of these

> brought inestimable gifts to the world, but they also brought great suffering, most notably but not exclusively to Jews. Like a tidal wave they swept away local customs, ancient traditions and different ways of doing things. They were to cultural diversity what industrialisation is to biodiversity. They extinguished weaker forms of life. They diminished difference.

We should note that Sacks is not unappreciative of these cultures, but he deplores their drive to universalize themselves at the expense of the particularity and diversity that they suppress.

This is Sacks' account of the significance of 9/11: 'September 11 happened when two universalist cultures – each profoundly threatening to the other – met and clashed.' He is not referring to Christianity here. In other words, Sacks does not perpetuate the common perception in the Muslim world (and of some westerners) that the west – the United States and her allies – represents Christianity in the world, so that the clash between the west and militant Islam is a clash between religious cultures, Christian and Muslim. That perception seriously mistakes the role of Christianity in the contemporary world. Jonathan Sacks correctly observes that in the west and its huge spheres of influence and power in the rest of the world we are now living under a sixth great universal order: global capitalism. This is a universal culture with a much more obviously universal base than its predecessors, but one in which an all-powerful economic system decisively influences all other aspects of life. According to Sacks, this universalist culture is

> the first to be driven not by a set of ideas but by a series of institutions, among them the market, the media and the Internet. But its effect is no less profound. It threatens all things local, traditional and particular.

His contrast between ideas and institutions here may be misleading: global capitalism surely has its driving ideas, a fundamentalist attachment to free-market economic liberalism, while ancient Rome and medieval Christendom certainly had powerful institutions. But Sacks is no doubt right that Islamic extremists who wish to destroy America correctly identify it with economic globalization, as well as military hegemony in the Middle East: hence the attack on the towers of the World Trade Center as well as on the Pentagon. With historical memories that include the Crusades, Islamic extremists doubtless see the economic and military dominance of the United States as the latest manifestation of Christian imperialism. But Islam also has traditionally had aspirations to universal dominance. Islam has always expected world history to issue – by God's design and human effort – in the umma, the universal success of Islam, the universal Islamic state, accommodating no other forms of belief or life. With the necessary and significant proviso that the deliberate slaughter of thousands of innocent civilians would not be an acceptable method for the majority of Muslims, there is something in Jonathan Sacks' claim that global capitalism and Islam are indeed profoundly threatening to each other, and that in some sense 11 September, with its continuing aftermath, represents their collision.

At this point we should pause in our consideration of Sacks' article in order to note that he is working with two concepts that we need to notice, because they are essential for understanding our contemporary world and also will be important for this book. They will be especially important when, in the last chapter, we return to the issues raised by Sacks, but they are also concepts it will be helpful to have in mind throughout. One of these is the notion of a metanarrative or grand narrative. Sacks' article does not use this term, but he is clearly reflecting the thinking of those who do. When he speaks of universalist cultures, cultures with an ideological drive to universalize themselves, he is talking about cultures that see the world in terms of a metanarrative, that is, a story about the meaning of reality as a whole, or at least human reality as a whole. A metanarrative is an attempt to grasp the meaning and destiny of human history as a whole by telling a single story about it; to encompass, as it were, all the immense diversity of human stories in a single, overall story which integrates them into a single meaning. Ancient Rome told a story about its worldwide empire, about the inclusion of all nations and cultures in the dominant empire of Rome, which meant peace and prosperity for all. Of course, it was an ideology that justified the self-serving power of Rome by a myth of universal benefit: the nations that Rome conquered for her own benefit were assured that they too would benefit. Moreover, the Roman Empire appealed to the Roman state gods for legitimation: its political myths were a sort of political theology. We see here the dangerous ambiguity of metanarratives, which often, certainly, serve to justify empire and oppression. We shall have to consider whether they always do so, but certainly it is true that they are all too often narratives of domination and oppression, dressing up the realities of exploitative power in claims to divine authorization and universal benefit.

Christianity and Islam are among the world religions that tell a story about the meaning of the whole of reality. The Bible, as we shall be taking very seriously in this book, tells a story that in some sense encompasses all other human stories, draws them into the meaning that God's story with the world gives them. Until the modern period all metanarratives were explicitly religious, but since the eighteenth century two great secular substitutes have become quite as dominant in the world as any world religion. These are the fifth and sixth in Jonathan Sacks' enumeration of universalist cultures. From the European Enlightenment stemmed the idea of progress, the great myth by which western modernity has lived. The idea of progress was a myth of universal history. It claimed that humanity is on a path of progress towards a better, ultimately Utopian future. The rationalist values of western secular modernity were taken to be universal values, so that their propagation was the natural good of all, and the supersession of all local cultures by the self-evident goods of western modernity was progress. The means of progress were education, technology and imperialism. Along with the sincerely benevolent spread of western values and technology went the massive harnessing of the resources of the rest of the world to the flourishing of the western nations. The metanarrative of progress was significantly a narrative of domination, for all that it made freedom one of its major values.

Marxism was for a long time an immensely powerful metanarrative, a variation on the Enlightenment idea of progress. But the so-called fall of communism has left much of the world clear for the ideology and domination of the west in a new form, Sacks' sixth universalist culture: global capitalism or economic globalization.

Globalization is the second of the two concepts that it is useful to introduce at this stage. As a general phenomenon, globalization describes the way the world is rapidly becoming a whole in which the parts interact and relate to each other, almost independently of geography. The modern media and the new information technology have much to do with this. But more specifically the phenomenon we are addressing is economic globalization or the dominance of global capitalism. This is undoubtedly a western-dominated process in which a purportedly universal ideology – unfettered free-market capitalism as a self-evident good – serves the economic interests of those with economic power. Globalization is the new imperialism, a purely economic rather than political imperialism. Globalization has succeeded the older idea of progress in that it reduces progress to economic growth, which is supposed to bring all other goods in its train. Globalization tells a story – and its success has a lot to do with the convincingness of this story – about the irresistible triumph of global capitalism, about the universalizing of the culture it promotes. This is the metanarrative that, according to Sacks, now clashes (not as it once did with the Marxist metanarrative, but now) with the much older metanarrative of militant Islam: two projects of world domination.

A critique of all metanarratives is integral to the intellectual and cultural movement known as postmodernism. For postmodern thinking, metanarratives (such as and especially the Enlightenment idea of progress) are typically modern. Postmodernism is reaction against, rejection of all, metanarratives, because as attempts to universalize one's own values or culture they are necessarily authoritarian or oppressive. Postmodernism exposes metanarratives as projects of power and domination. In place of such universal pretensions postmodernism opts for particularity, diversity, localism, relativism. This postmodern critique of metanarratives is also something to which we shall return in the last chapter of this book.

We can now return to Jonathan Sacks' article and the lesson he draws from the adverse effects, as he sees them, of the universalizing nature of the universal cultures and their metanarratives. As Chief Rabbi he is naturally concerned with the religious dimension of this, and here is his Jewish, rather postmodern, conclusion from his observations:

> [U]niversalism is the cultural counterpart of imperialism. Not all truth is universal. Scientific truth is. Spiritual, religious and at least some moral truth is not ... To put it another way, there is a fundamental difference between God and religion. God is universal, religion is particular. We serve God, author of diversity, by respecting diversity. God no more wants all faiths and cultures to be the same than a loving parent wants his or her children to be the same ... We will make peace in this troubled world only when we learn that God loves difference and so, at last, must we.

There is much here to give us pause for thought. It is illuminating to compare, for example, the Taliban's destruction of the unique Buddhist rock-carved statues in Afghanistan, which appalled the western world, with the ever-increasing threat to local cultures throughout the non-western world created by the so-called Coca-colonization of the world, the relentless universalization of commercialized American culture. If militant Islam at its worst treats cultural diversity with contempt, repression and vandalism, so does economic globalization, even if it often does so by taking up local culture, commercializing and marketing it, absorbing it into its own economic monoculture, but preserving only what it can turn into commodities for profit.

But where does Christianity stand in all this? Where does Christianity stand between the universalist ambitions of McWorld and Jihad? Because it is often forgotten, it is worth noting initially the remarkable cultural diversity of Christianity in its many historical and contemporary manifestations. When Ninian Smart wrote a book called *The Phenomenon of Christianity* he aimed in part to illustrate this diversity of worldwide Christianity to readers who unthinkingly assume that all Christianity is much the same as the kind they know. He began the book with the Orthodox church in Romania, no doubt to defamiliarize such readers from the start. 'Christianity', he claimed, 'is not a single thing, but a kaleidoscope of different lived interpretations of faith.'[1] And to make the point from some of the examples he goes on to describe, he asks:

> What do the Amish of Pennsylvania have in common with a Zulu Zion? What does [Lutheran] Sweden share with the old faith of Ethiopia? What transition is to be made from the Catholicism of Lombardy to the Baptism [he means the Baptist churches] of Georgia [USA] or the Calvinism of the Voortrekkers [the Afrikaners of South Africa]?[2]

Of course, he does not deny that they do have something in common, and he explores the commonality in the last chapter of his book through examining the differences between Christianity and other world faiths. But his book is a useful reminder that, whatever defines Christianity as a historical world phenomenon, cultural homogeneity

---

[1] N. Smart, *The Phenomenon of Christianity* (London: Collins, 1979), p. 7.

[2] Ibid., p. 11.

is not likely to be such a feature. Almost certainly Christianity exhibits more cultural diversity than any other religion, and that must say something about it.

However, this is not really to grasp the nettle of the Chief Rabbi's assertion that 'there is a fundamental difference between God and religion. God is universal, religion is particular.' Can this be true? Pursue it just a few simple steps of further argument and one quickly runs into the familiar problem that there is rather little in common between the beliefs about God of the various religions (taken inclusively rather than limited to those that have more in common). Therefore what the religions believe about God belongs to their particularity rather than to God's universality. Since not all religions believe that God is the Creator of all things, is this statement, apparently about the universality of God, in fact only an aspect of the particularity of Judaism, Christianity, Islam and a few other religions that make it? While the distinction between God as universal and religion as particular is highly appealing to many people in the contemporary west at least, trying to come to terms with the religious pluralism of their own societies and the world, it is hard to maintain without lapsing into sheer relativism: that any truth is as good as any other. I think we must start somewhere else. If we wish to speak of the biblical God (as Rabbi Sacks undoubtedly does), then we must say: *God* is both universal and particular. The God of the Jewish Scriptures is both the God who made heaven and earth and the God of Abraham, Isaac and Jacob; both the God whose loving purpose is at work in all the nations and the God who chose Israel alone and chose to identify himself actually to the other nations as the God of Israel; both the God who fills heaven and earth and the God who dwells in the midst of his own people. It is not at all that the universal aspect applies only to God and the particular only to religion. Both are genuinely true of God. We do not find God by abstracting God from the particularities of God's history with Israel. We find the universal God in his particularity as the God of Israel and (Christians may add to what Jonathan Sacks might say) also as the God of Jesus.

I have taken this route into the subject of this book because the issue of universality and particularity is essential to what I shall say about mission and what I shall say about the way the Bible invites us to read it. The Bible has its own understanding of the relationship between the particular and the universal, and it is in that relationship that the church's universal mission belongs and has meaning. Mission is a sending from the one human person Jesus Christ into all the world as his witnesses. Mission takes place on the way from the particularity of God's action in the story of Jesus to the universal coming of God's kingdom. It happens as particular people called by God go from here to there and live for God here and there for the sake of all people. But Jonathan Sacks' argument obliges us to face some hard questions about this movement from the particular to the universal. Is it indeed 'a tidal wave' of religious homogenization sweeping away all the diversity of the world? Is it a kind of ecclesiastical imperialism or ecclesiastical globalization, that should be subject to exactly the kind of critique postmodernism applies to the Enlightenment, anti-colonialism to western imperialism, or anti-globalizing protesters to economic globalization? Does it, we might say, in its drive to universalize one particular suppress and eliminate all other particulars? Is it, in this sense, what postmodern jargon calls a 'totalizing' movement – perhaps a more accurate expression than Sacks' 'universalist culture' for the same phenomenon he describes? Facing these hard questions, as we will in the last chapter of this book, may help us to distinguish biblical mission from its distortions, and perhaps to get our Christian bearings in the world as 9/11 and its consequences have rather unexpectedly revealed it. But for the time being we must turn to the biblical narrative.

2. Outlines of a hermeneutic for the kingdom of God

This book is not an account of what the Bible says about mission or a biblical theology of mission. There is a lot to be said about mission in the Bible that will not be said here. The purpose of this book is more hermeneutical. In other words, it is about how to read the Bible in a way that takes seriously its missionary direction.[3] I shall try to show how the Bible itself embodies a kind of movement from the particular to the universal, which we as readers need to find ourselves inside. The Bible is a kind of project aimed at the kingdom of God, that is, towards the achievement of God's purposes for good in the whole of God's creation. This is a universal direction that takes the particular with the utmost seriousness. Christian communities or individuals are always setting off from the particular as both the Bible and our own situation defines it and following the biblical direction towards the universal that is to be found not apart from but within other particulars. This is mission.

What sort of hermeneutic will enable us to enter into the Bible's own missionary direction from the particular to the universal? It must be, in the first place, a canonical

---

[3] Another recent argument for a missionary hermeneutic is H. D. Beeby, 'A Missional Approach to Renewed Interpretation' in C. Bartholomew, C. Greene and K. Möller (eds), *Renewing Biblical Interpretation* (Carlisle/Grand Rapids, Michigan: Paternoster/Zondervan, 2000), pp. 268–83. His emphases are different from but complementary to mine.

hermeneutic, that is, a way of reading the Bible as a whole. Secondly, it will be a narrative hermeneutic, one which recognizes how the Bible as a whole tells a story, in some sense a single story, an overall narrative encompassing, of course, many other stories and including many forms of non-narrative literature within it, but constituting in its overall direction a metanarrative, a narrative about the whole of reality that elucidates the meaning of the whole of reality. A narrative hermeneutic recognizes the way narrative creates its own world in front of the text and so interprets our world for us; how narrative opens up new possibilities of living that change us and our world; how we are given our identities by the narratives of our own lives and the wider narratives to which they relate. To focus on the narrative character of the Bible not only does justice to the character of the Bible; it also makes possible a hermeneutic that connects with the character of people's experience. Stories come naturally to people. The human world, it has been said, is story-shaped.[4] We all instinctively understand the world by telling stories about it. If the Bible offers a metanarrative, a story of all stories, then we should all be able to place our own stories within that grand narrative and find our own perception and experience of the world transformed by that connexion.

This book's proposal of a hermeneutic for the kingdom of God involves, as I have already suggested, a focus on one prominent aspect of the narrative shape of the biblical story: its movement from the particular to the universal. As I have also briefly suggested, this direction of the biblical story corresponds to the biblical God, who is the God of the one people Israel and the one human being Jesus Christ, and is also the Creator and LORD of all things. We can better appreciate this universality and

---

[4] B. Wicker, *The Story-Shaped World* (London: Athlone Press, 1975).

particularity of God himself when we recognize that this biblical God's own identity is itself a *narrative* identity. It is a particular identity God gives himself in the particular story of Israel and Jesus, and it is an identity which itself drives the narrative towards the universal realization of God's kingdom in all creation. God identifies himself as the God of Abraham, Israel and Jesus *in order to be* the God of all people and the Lord of all things. Moreover, in the narrative world of the Bible the people of God is also given its identity in this movement from the particular to the universal, an identity whose God-given dynamic we commonly sum up in the word 'mission'. God, God's people and God's world are related to each other primarily in a narrative that mediates constantly the particular and the universal.

If we look more closely at the movement of the biblical narrative from the particular to the universal we can see that it has three aspects or three dimensions: the temporal, the spatial and the social. We shall now take a preliminary look at each of these. In each case we shall find that what we say about the biblical narrative implies something significant about mission.

(1) The *temporal* movement of the biblical narrative runs all the way from creation to the eschatological future. It runs from the old to the new, constantly reconstructing the past in memory and constructing the future in expectation. Within this movement mission is movement into the new future of God. It is the movement of the people of God whose identity is found in the narrative of the past but also in their being turned by that narrative towards the coming of God's kingdom in the future. The possibilities the narrative opens up for them, when they find themselves in it, are those God gives as they live towards God's future. Temporally, then, *mission is movement into the ever-new future.*

Temporal movement is not as such necessarily from the particular to the universal, but in the case of the biblical narrative it is. From Genesis 12 to Revelation the narrative is always in transition from a particular past towards the universal future. This is so definitively in the movement from the history of Jesus to his future coming and the coming of the kingdom of God in all creation. It is Jesus' life, death and resurrection that open up God's new future for all creation, and so it is only as the universal future of Jesus, as the future projected by his particular story, that the New Testament knows the future. Mission is the movement that takes place between Jesus' own sending by his Father and the future coming of Jesus in the kingdom of his Father.

(2) The *spatial* (or geographical) movement of the biblical narrative runs from one place to every place, from the centre to the periphery, from Jerusalem to the ends of the earth. This too is the divine movement of God's saving purpose from his particular presence in the Temple in the midst of his own people Israel towards the coming of his universal kingdom. The church finds its identity also within this geographical movement. Spatially, then, *mission is movement towards ever-new horizons*.

We shall discuss this geographical aspect of mission in more detail in the next chapter. Biblical scholars who usually take history seriously have rarely taken geography equally seriously, but literal and theological geography forms a very significant aspect of the biblical narrative. The philosopher Paul Ricoeur wrote a seminal study called *Time and Narrative*, of which a hermeneutic for the kingdom of God requires a biblical-theological version. But it also requires a biblical-theological version of Ricoeur's non-existent *Space and Narrative* – non-existent no doubt because philosophy and literary studies have also usually been more interested in time and history than in space and place.

(3) Movement in time and space is also movement of people, movement from person to person, from people to people. The Old Testament typically reckons time in genealogies, and the New Testament measures space in journeys. Both are means of measuring by human movement, by contrast with the inhumanly abstract measures the modern world favours. The social or, we could say, numerical movement of the biblical narrative is from the one to the many, from Abraham to the nations, from Jesus to every creature in heaven, on earth and under the earth. Socially, then, *mission is a movement that is always being joined by others, the movement, therefore, of an ever-new people.*

The movement of the biblical narrative thus moves from the particular to the universal in all three dimensions of time, space and human sociality. Many specific stories in the Bible portray instances of this movement from the particular towards the universal in all three of its aspects. Abraham surveys the land his descendants will one day populate. Ruth the Moabite throws in her lot with her mother-in-law and her mother-in-law's people and God: she finds a new future, in a new land, among a new people. The prophet Elisha sends the whole Syrian army home with not a drop of blood shed. King Nebuchadnezzar recovers his reason and with it the knowledge that God's is the only truly universal and eternal kingdom. Elizabeth and Mary, the two mothers-to-be, celebrate the future with which they are pregnant. Jesus dines with the tax collectors, cleanses the lepers and raises the dead. Simon of Cyrene shares the burden of his cross and the centurion intuits his crucified identity. Phoebe prepares Paul's way to Rome and Onesimus returns to his master, now his Christian brother. These examples have been chosen almost at random. Once we grasp the threefold movement of God's purpose we shall readily find it instantiated in endlessly varying ways from Genesis to Revelation. In order to understand the relationship of particularity and universality in Scripture we need to keep in focus both the unique particularities of all of these stories and also the universal horizon to which they are oriented by their place in the overall metanarrative of Scripture.

A metanarrative of this kind has a definite future goal towards which it moves. The actual *attainment* of this goal, the point at which the fully universal is reached, the end of the story, cannot of course be portrayed in historical narrative, for it is still future, or even in realistic fictional narrative, since it anticipates an end that surpasses anything in the realistic world we can describe. The realistic narratives of Scripture can portray only the ever-recurrent setting out from the particular towards the universal in a movement which can move in a universal direction only by way of other particulars, since the goal is not an abstract universal but the gathering of all particulars into the one kingdom of the one God. This goal itself is portrayed not in realistic narrative but in a rich variety of narrative metaphors and images. We can sample these now by attending to three to be found in the Gospels, each of the three representing one of the three aspects of the movement: temporal, spatial and social.

(1) Our first example is Jesus' parable of the seed that grows by itself:

> The kingdom of God is as if someone would scatter seed on the ground, and would sleep and rise night and day, and the seed would sprout and grow, he does not know how. The earth produces of itself, first the stalk, then the head, then the full grain in the head. But when the grain is ripe, at once

he goes in with his sickle, because the harvest has come.

(Mark 4:26–29, NRSV)

Here the most prominent aspect is the temporal. While the farmer lives his normal life from day to day, the seed he has sown sprouts and grows until the moment for harvest – a common biblical image of the eschatological consummation – arrives. He does not know how it grows. Jewish farmers in first-century Palestine would think less of a process of natural cause and effect, more of an annual miracle, the direct act of God's power and generosity, as in Paul's observation that he planted and Apollos watered, but it was God who gave the growth (1 Corinthians 3:6). From the seed planted in Jesus' ministry to the eschatological harvest, the movement is not humanly calculable or achievable, but the gift of God. The church in its missionary vocation is not so much the agent of the process as the product of the process on the way to its God-given goal.

(2) The parable of the mustard seed (Mark 4:30–33 and parallels) employs another of the agricultural images so characteristic of Jesus' parables:

With what can we compare the kingdom of God, or what parable will we use for it? It is like a mustard seed, which, when sown upon the ground, is the smallest of all the seeds on earth; yet when it is sown it grows up and becomes the greatest of all shrubs, and puts forth large branches, so that the birds of the air can make nests in its shade.

(Mark 4:30–33, NRSV)

At first glance this parable may seem to convey the same message as the parable of the seed growing by itself, but in fact it has its own distinctive nuance. Here it is the spatial aspect that is stressed, in the contrast between the smallest of all seeds and the greatest of all shrubs into which it grows. The sizeable shrub that the mustard plant actually is is so described as to evoke the image of the mythological world tree, which from its trunk at the centre of the world overshadows the whole world with its branches. In Daniel (4:10–12) and Ezekiel (17:22–23) this was already an image of God's universal kingdom, the birds in its branches representing the nations that enjoy the blessings of God's rule. Here it is not the process of growth that is the point, but the fact that the insignificant beginnings will lead to the astonishingly great end result. No more than in the case of our first parable should we assimilate this parable to a modern ideology of progress. We should not, as it were, place ourselves at some point in the seed's steady growth to world tree proportions. The church is never far from the insignificance of Jesus and his band of unimpressive followers. It is always setting out from the particular in the direction of God's incalculable gift of everything.

(3) The third parabolic story (or stories) from the gospels is an acted parable: the miraculous catch of fish, which in both Luke (5:1–11) and John (21:2–11) is intended to illustrate Jesus' designation of the disciples as fishers of people:

> Gathered there together were Simon Peter, Thomas called the Twin, Nathanael of Cana in Galilee, the sons of Zebedee, and two others of his disciples. Simon Peter said to them, 'I am going fishing.' They said to him, 'We will go with you.' They went out and got into the boat, but that night they caught nothing. Just after daybreak, Jesus stood on the beach; but the disciples did not know that it was Jesus. Jesus said to them, 'Children, you have no fish, have you?' They answered him; 'No.' He said to them, 'Cast the net to the right side of the boat, and you will find some.' So

they cast it, and now they were not able to haul it in because there were so many fish. That disciple whom Jesus loved said to Peter, 'It is the Lord!' When Simon Peter heard that it was the Lord, he put on some clothes, for he was naked, and jumped into the sea. But the other disciples came in the boat, dragging the net full of fish, for they were not far from the land, only about a hundred yards off ... Jesus said to them, 'Bring some of the fish that you have just caught.' So Simon Peter went aboard and hauled the net ashore, full of large fish, a hundred fifty-three of them; and though there were so many, the net was not torn.

(John 21:2–8, 10–11, NRSV)

In the epilogue to John's Gospel this fishing story serves a similar function to that of the great commission at the end of Matthew and Luke. It previews the church's mission that lies ahead of the gospel narrative itself. Also in John the emphasis is on the social or numerical aspect of the metanarrative movement: the fishing disciples are 7 (the number of completeness) and so representative of all, while the catch is counted and numbers 153 fish. If it is correct to understand this number as the number of kinds of fish there are,[5] it suggests the inclusion of people of all nations in the church, but in any case it suggests a remarkably large number. Unlike the two parables of growth, in this case the activity of the church itself in the movement from particular to universal is pictured in the story. It is represented by the fishing activity of the disciples. But the fishing is futile until Jesus intervenes. The results of mission are always the gift of God.

---

[5] This was Jerome's explanation, but his statement that the Greek biologists reckoned 153 kinds of fish is open to question: for this and other explanations, see R. E. Brown, *The Gospel According to John* (AB; London: Chapman, 1971), pp. 1074–6.

In these three examples we see how the church's mission takes place between its commissioning by God and the coming of the kingdom of God. It lives from the God who gives and sends and towards the God who gives and comes. We can see how the world of possibilities the biblical narratives create for their readers is not simply a different way of seeing the world, though it is that, nor are the possibilities such as the church's mission itself can achieve. The missionary church's 'passion for the possible' (to borrow the philosopher Ernst Bloch's phrase) is a passion for what is possible with God, for what the church, living faithfully and expectantly, receives as divine gift in every anticipation of the coming kingdom.

We have also noted the very significant point that the movement from the particular to the universal in which the church's mission belongs should not be confused with the progressivism of the modern world. This has been the characteristic error of western modernity, and too often the church in the modern period has confused its mission with the modern metanarrative of progress. But this secular doctrine of progress, a secular substitute for biblical eschatology, has dissolved before our eyes during the second half of the twentieth century, a century described by George Steiner as 'the most bestial in recorded history'.[6] Progressivist doctrines of mission were all too obviously, we can now see, either tied up with the modern Enlightenment philosophy of human progress or religious reflections of it. Apart from anything else, they dispel the ambiguities and obscurities of real history with a far too ambitious attempt to discern the purpose of God in historical patterns that are there for all to see. They are also triumphalist in tendency, apt

---

[6] G. Steiner, *Errata: An Examined Life* (London: Weidenfeld & Nicolson, 1997), p. 103.

to obscure the fact that genuinely Christian mission is witness to the crucified Christ.

So the church's mission is not a steadily cumulative process in which we move ever further away from the biblical narratives. We are always beginning again from the biblical narratives, which still open up unexpected possibilities for our own future within the future of Jesus Christ. We are always figuratively starting again from Jerusalem on our way to the ends of the earth. We are always starting again from Jesus who is the one human for all others, and we are always starting again from Pentecost, the event that gives birth to the new community on its way to the new future.

3. Anticipated closure and permanent narrative openness

There is a further and rather surprising aspect of the way the New Testament speaks of the universal goal of God's and the church's mission. Its language sometimes strongly suggests that this universal goal has been almost or even already achieved at the time of writing. Taking up again our three aspects of the movement from particular to universal, it seems the New Testament indulges in temporal, geographical and numerical hyperbole. In the first place, *temporally*, as is well known, New Testament writers anticipate the coming of Jesus in glory in the near future. Paul habitually assumes he and his readers will be alive at the parousia (1 Thessalonians 4:15, 17; 1 Corinthians 15:51; 1 Timothy 6:13–14), even though he is also quite capable of reckoning with his possible death (2 Corinthians 5:1–5; Philippians 1:20–26). Secondly, *geographically*, Paul can tell the Roman Christians that their 'faith is proclaimed throughout the whole world'

(Romans 1:8), even though he was particularly conscious when writing Romans that there were not yet churches even in parts of the Roman Empire. He makes comparable claims elsewhere, amounting to a habit of geographical exaggeration that is less easily explained than the temporal one (1 Thessalonians 1:8; Colossians 1:6; 2 Corinthians 2:14; cf. 1 Peter 5:9). Moreover, *socially or numerically*, in Colossians 1:23 Paul can claim that the gospel 'has been proclaimed to every creature under heaven'.[7] These Pauline hyperboles are not just 'rhetorical' but express the urgent dynamic of the gospel towards its universal goal and Paul's overwhelming sense of his personal vocation within that dynamic.

Nor is such hyperbole confined to Paul. All three forms of hyperbole – temporal, spatial and numerical – are especially evident in the book of Revelation if we read it as its first readers would have done, addressed to themselves in their own time and place. In some respects the hyperboles of the book of Revelation parallel the Roman Empire's patently exaggerated claim to rule the world – exaggerated not because of our own knowledge of

---

[7] Even after the most careful explanations of how this phrase could be justified by Paul's strategy of planting the gospel in places from which it is to spread and his realistic hope of completing the mission to the Gentiles in his lifetime (see H. Stettler, 'An Interpretation of Colossians 1:24 in the Framework of Paul's Mission Theology' in J. Ådna and H. Kvalbein (eds), *The Mission of the Early Church to Jews and Gentiles* [Tübingen: Mohr Siebeck, 2000], pp. 207–8), 'a degree of hyperbole cannot be denied' (J. D. G. Dunn, *The Epistles to the Colossians and to Philemon* [NIGTC; Grand Rapids, Michigan/ Carlisle: Eerdmans/Paternoster, 1996], p. 112). The poorly attested variant reading that inserts τη (giving the meaning 'in the whole creation') is presumably an attempt to reduce the hyperbole. The hyperbole is less difficult when we set it in the context of similar forms of hyperbole in Paul, as we have suggested in the main text.

continents unknown to the ancients, but because much of the well-known world of the time lay beyond the empire's borders. Much as the Roman Empire's pagan political theology required the claim to universal rule, so the early church's eagerness for the coming universal kingdom of God found expression in hyperbole. Just as the beast rules over 'every tribe and people and language and nation' (13:7), so the church is drawn from 'every tribe and language and people and nation' (5:9) and its message goes out to 'every nation and tribe and language and people' (14:6). Whereas the empire claims immortality, invincibility and eternal rule (13:3–4; 18:7), Revelation allows the beast only a little while yet (17:10) and echoes from start to finish with the expectation, urgent, admonitory and encouraging, that the time is near (1:3; 22:10) and the Lord Jesus is coming soon (3:1; 22:7, 12, 20). Is this anticipated closure of history a kind of *premature* closure of the openness of history? Are all the options already closed off in this hyperbolic drawing of the end results into the immediate present?

We can give a negative answer to such questions if we also attend to the way the New Testament's narrative of the church's mission in the New Testament period noticeably stops short of its universal goal. In terms of narrative function, we could say that it stops short at the point where we come in. A comparison with the Old Testament may be helpful. The Pentateuch or Torah, the foundation story of Israel, ends, perhaps rather surprisingly, just before the people of Israel enter the land of Canaan and take possession of it. Some interpreters explain this by supposing that the Pentateuch reached its final form in the period of the Babylonian exile and for this reason ends its story of the Israelites of old at a point comparable with the position of the Israelites in Babylon, poised to re-enter and to repossess the promised land.[8] Similarly, we might say, the New Testament narrative leaves the task of mission incomplete, as it has been for every generation of its readers. Paul's intention of going on from Rome to Spain is not fulfilled, at least within the pages of Scripture. It is very striking that the Acts of the Apostles ends in a peculiarly open and inconclusive way, simply with Paul continuing to preach the gospel. Has the gospel now reached the end of the earth, as Jesus' commission at the beginning of Acts (1:8) requires? Certainly not. Has Israel's permanent response to the gospel been made, as many interpreters of Acts, wanting Luke to settle a question he constantly raises throughout his work, wish to suppose?[9] No, nothing is concluded at the end of Acts, not even Paul's own ministry. Everything is left unconcluded – that is, the story ends where every generation of readers down to ourselves comes in.

Moreover the statements of universality often quite patently reach far beyond the narrative horizons of the New Testament. Paul's remarkable statement that in Christ 'there is no longer Greek and Jew ... barbarian [and] Scythian' (Colossians 3:11) opens up a whole vista of as yet unevangelized savages (for as savages, worse than barbarians, Scythians were conventionally regarded) in the little-known northern reaches of the world beyond the Black Sea. The 'great multitude that no one could count, from every nation, from all tribes and peoples and languages' – depicted in Revelation 7 – is far from the reality of the church at the end of the first century, when the number of Christians probably could have been

---

[8] J. A. Sanders, *Torah and Canon* (Philadelphia: Fortress, 1972).

[9] On this point, see R. Bauckham, 'The Restoration of Israel in Luke-Acts' in J. M. Scott (ed.), *Restoration: Old Testament, Jewish and Christian Perspectives* (JSJSS 72; Leiden: Brill, 2001), pp. 435–87.

counted at least as accurately as the Jewish historian Josephus numbers the Essenes and the Pharisees. Moreover, the New Testament does not map out in advance the twists and turns of history, the particular narrative or narratives that will take place between its narrative present and its symbolic and metaphorical expressions of the universal goal of the kingdom. Of course, it characterizes in various ways the permanent or recurrent kinds of situations in which the church will find itself and in which its mission must be pursued. But these are generalities, not particulars. Precisely by anticipating the universal goal so immediately, the New Testament leaves very widely open all the penultimates of history. It does not, as so many Christians down the ages have wanted it to do, give the church in any particular time a specific temporal position in a predicted sequence of history leading from then to the parousia. Rather it puts all its readers where its first readers stood – between the church's commissioning by Jesus and the future coming of Jesus. The New Testament gives the church in every age its missionary identity by plunging it into the midst of the biblical story where the words of the great commission still ring in its ears.

In conclusion to this topic, we may say that the New Testament puts the church in its missionary situation in a dialectic of anticipated closure and permanent openness. This means that the universal goal of God's purpose for the world presses upon us with a kind of immediacy that impacts the church's life and mission. It keeps us aware that it is God's purpose for the whole world and the whole of history that is at work and with which we are involved. At the same time the universality may not override the particular, as though, in some grand universal strategy, the church were to ignore the particularities of its context here and there. The local narratives generated by the Bible's story here and there, in this or that specific context, as the church seeks to live faithfully to its commission in the particularities which belong to it and in which it finds itself at any time or place, are all unique. As the New Testament illustrates so profusely, the movement towards the universal is always from one particular to another. Even the great universal drama of the Bible's final book is accessible only through the particularities of the seven churches of Asia, their situation and their practice, specified with such attention to the particular, in the introduction to that book (Revelation 1–3).

Chapter 2

From the One to the Many

The purpose of this chapter is to show that the notion of a movement of the biblical narrative from the particular to the universal helps us to see what is going on in that narrative when we attempt to read it holistically. We shall focus on perhaps the most important forms that this movement takes: four different strands in the biblical metanarrative. The first three share a common pattern; the fourth is different and distinctive.

In the first three cases, God's purpose begins with a singular choice: God singles out first Abraham, then Israel, then David. The three movements that begin with these three choices by God each has its own distinctive theme, one aspect of God's purpose for the world. We could call these the thematic trajectories of the narrative. The trajectory that moves from Abraham to all the families of the earth is the trajectory of blessing. The trajectory that moves from Israel to all the nations is the trajectory of God's revelation of himself to the world. The trajectory that moves from God's enthronement of David in Zion to the ends of the earth is the trajectory of rule, of God's kingdom coming in all creation. Of course, these three movements and themes are closely interrelated.

1. From Abraham to all the families of the earth

In Genesis 12 Abraham is *singled out* by God. This is perhaps the most remarkable of all the instances of divinely chosen singularity in the Bible. For it follows immediately the thoroughly universal narrative of the first eleven chapters of Genesis, a narrative that concluded, in chapter 10, with the great catalogue of all the nations, seventy of them, descended from the three sons of Noah, and then, in chapter 11, with the story of Babel, from which the human race was scattered over all the earth to form the various nations, divided now by language and geography. Genesis 10–11 sets, as it were, the international scene for the whole of the rest of the Bible's story. But from this emphatically universal scope the story suddenly narrows to just the one man, Abraham, and his immediate family, called by God to leave his place in the international order (or disorder), to move to a new country and into a new future of which he knows only from God.

However, we also learn at once that this singling out of Abraham from all the nations is not at all to be understood as God's giving up on the nations. This is not like the choice of Noah and his family, when the rest of humanity perished in the flood, and Noah's descendants replaced them. In Abraham's case he is singled out precisely so that blessing may come to all the nations,[1] to all those seventy nations God had scattered over the face of the whole earth. Blessing is the key word in God's

---

[1] For the blessing of the nations as the ultimate purpose of God's call of Abraham, according to Genesis 12:2–3, see P. D. Miller, 'Syntax and Theology in Genesis xii 3a', *Vetus Testamentum* 34 (1984), pp. 472–5. For a careful recent study of the promise in Genesis 12:2–3, see J. Bailey Wells, *God's Holy People: A Theme in Biblical Theology* (JSOTSS 305; Sheffield: Sheffield Academic Press, 2000), pp. 185–207.

promises to Abraham: Abraham himself will be blessed, in that his descendants will be a great nation, and Abraham will be a blessing, in that all the families of the earth[2] will be blessed (Genesis 12:2–3).[3] From the one man Abraham and the one new nation that descends from him, God's blessing will overflow to all other nations.

The promise that all the nations will be blessed is repeated four more times in Genesis (18:18; 22:18; 26:4; 28:14). On the last two of these occasions it is given to Abraham's son Isaac and grandson Jacob. Moreover,

---

[2] Bailey Wells, *God's Holy People*, p. 204: '"Family" ... suggests a grouping intermediate between a tribe and a father's house, a "clan".'

[3] On the alternative translations, 'in you all the families of the earth shall be blessed' and 'by you all the families of the earth shall bless themselves' (NRSV and NRSV margin respectively), see J. Scharbert, 'brk' in G. J. Botterweck and H. Ringgren (eds), *Theological Dictionary of the Old Testament*, J. T. Willis (tr.) (Grand Rapids, Michigan: Eerdmans, 1975), vol. 2, p. 297; Bailey Wells, *God's Holy People*, pp. 203–6; C. Westermann, *Genesis 12–36*, J. J. Scullion (tr.) (London: SPCK, 1985), pp. 151–2, who comments: 'the reflexive translation ["shall bless themselves"] is saying no less than the passive or receptive. When "the families of the earth bless" themselves "in Abraham", i.e. call a blessing on themselves under the invocation of his name ... then the obvious presupposition is that they receive the blessing ... Where the name of Abraham is spoken in a prayer for blessing, the blessing of Abraham streams forth; it knows no bounds and reaches all the families of the earth' (p. 152). Bailey Wells, on the other hand, stresses the difference between the reflexive and the passive interpretations, both of which are possible, and distinguishes the reflexive interpretation as the meaning within the Hebrew Bible, the passive as the meaning when the promise is appropriated in the New Testament, though she notes that the passive meaning is adopted by the Septuagint (pp. 205–6). It is a pity she does not discuss the echoes of Genesis 12:2–3 within the Old Testament.

even within the stories of Jacob and his sons, the blessing of the nations begins – or at least is foreshadowed – when Jacob brings blessing to Laban (30:27) and Joseph to Potiphar (39:5). Then there is the peculiarly significant scene when the aged patriarch Jacob on his arrival in Egypt gives no less than the Egyptian Pharaoh his blessing (47:7). For the canonical reader Genesis creates a strong expectation that the blessing of the nations through Abraham's descendants is to be the goal of the rest of the biblical story. But in fact for the rest of the Old Testament story it remains no more than a promise and even as promise drops largely out of view. Only three or four passages in the rest of the Hebrew Bible echo this Abrahamic promise of blessing for the nations (Psalm 72:17;[4] Isaiah 19:24–25; Jeremiah 4:2; Zechariah 8:13).[5] This is an example of the unsystematic, even fragile, way in which a biblical metanarrative is formed out of the varied contents of the canon (a point to which we shall return in the last chapter). But the four echoes are significant, and we shall look at two of them.

The first is Jeremiah 4:1–2, in which the prophet is entreating Israel to repent of her faithlessness and return to the covenant with YHWH:

If you return, O Israel, says the LORD,
   if you return to me,
   if you remove your abominations from my presence

---

[4] Commentators do not generally recognize an echo of Genesis 12:3 here, but it was seen by the Septuagint translator, whose Greek here corresponds exactly to that of Genesis 12:3 LXX.

[5] Numbers 24:9b corresponds to Genesis 12:3a (cf. also Genesis 27:29b), but Balaam's oracles deal exclusively with the cursing of Israel's enemies, not the blessing of the nations. There are echoes elsewhere of the parts of the promises to Abraham that concern Israel alone, e.g. Deuteronomy 9:5; Psalm 105:8–11, but not of the promise of blessing for the nations.

and do not waver,
and if you swear, 'As the LORD lives!'
in truth, in justice, and in righteousness,
then nations shall be blessed [or: shall bless themselves][6]
   by him,
and by him they shall boast.

(NRSV)

What is notable here is that it is Israel's fulfilment of her covenant obligations, her practice of truth, justice and righteousness, that will bring blessing to the nations (cf. Genesis 18:18–19). In order for the nations to be blessed Israel need only be faithful to YHWH. Her life with YHWH will itself draw the nations to YHWH so that they too may experience his blessing. This brief reference to the promise of blessing for the nations is surely rather significant in the context of this book of a 'prophet to the nations' (1:5, cf. 10), whose prophecies are extensively concerned with the nations (chapters 46–51). It suggests that not only Israel's future, but the future of the nations also, could have been different from the judgements Jeremiah so relentlessly and agonizingly foresees. Blessing could have overflowed from faithful Israel to her national neighbours.

Secondly, the most remarkable echo of Genesis 12:3 outside Genesis is Isaiah 19:24–25. The prophet here expects in the future a kind of international federation of friendly powers: Israel herself and the two superpowers to the north and the south of her, Assyria and Egypt,

---

[6] The following line suggests that in this case the ambiguous verb is better translated 'shall bless themselves'. The point is that if Israel invokes YHWH while practising truth, justice and righteousness, then the nations will also invoke YHWH in blessing and boasting. But, of course, this entails also YHWH's blessing of the nations.

hitherto intransigent enemies, now at peace through their common worship of Israel's God:

> On that day Israel will be the third with Egypt and Assyria, a blessing in the midst of the earth, whom the LORD of hosts has blessed, saying, 'Blessed be Egypt my people, and Assyria the work of my hands, and Israel my heritage.'
>
> (NRSV)

Here Israel, from her central position 'in the midst of the earth' (a theme we shall take up in the next chapter), proves a blessing to her former oppressors, her international neighbours, and perhaps we are to understand that the blessing extends to all the nations since all could be envisaged as members of these three great empires. This is God's promise to Abraham coming to remarkably unexpected fruition. But, most remarkably of all, Israel's special status as YHWH's own covenant people is paralleled here by that of Egypt called here by God 'my people' and Assyria called by God 'the work of my hands'.[7] In this respect this is a vision echoed in the penultimate chapter of the Bible, where the prophet John sees the new Jerusalem descend from heaven in the new creation and hears it said:

> Behold, the dwelling of God is with humans.
> He will dwell with them as their God:
>   they will be his peoples, and God himself will be with them.
>
> (Revelation 21:3, NRSV altered)

While God's promise to Abraham is only rarely echoed in the Old Testament outside Genesis, it finds some significant echoes in the New Testament. Here Paul interprets the promise to mean that one specific descendant of Abraham, Jesus Christ, will bring blessing to Israel and

---

[7] This term is otherwise used to refer to a nation only in Isaiah 60:21, where the nation is Israel.

to all the nations (Galatians 3:6–9, 16).[8] Indeed, Paul identifies this promise as actually the Gospel:

> The Scripture, foreseeing that God would justify the Gentiles by faith, declared the gospel beforehand to Abraham, saying, 'All the Gentiles shall be blessed in you' [Genesis 12:3; 18:18]. For this reason, those who believe are blessed with Abraham who believed.
>
> (Galatians 3:8–9, NRSV)

Less often noticed is the way the Gospel of Matthew interprets the promise to Abraham in the same way that Paul does. Matthew frames the whole story of Jesus between the identification of him as a descendant of Abraham in the opening verse of the Gospel and, in the closing words of Jesus at the end of the Gospel, the commission to the disciples of Jesus to make disciples of all nations. Matthew's genealogy of Jesus begins with Abraham (1:1–2), not with Adam, as Luke's does (3:38), nor with David, which would have been sufficient to portray Jesus the Messiah the son of David, which certainly is an important theme in Matthew's Gospel. However, for Matthew, Jesus is the Messiah not only for Jews but also for Gentiles. He is the descendant of Abraham through whom God's blessing will at last reach the nations. Matthew's genealogy resumes the whole Old Testament story from Abraham onwards and continues, in a single line of father-to-son descent, until it reaches one descendant of Abraham, once again *singling out* one person from whom God's purpose of blessing will reach both Israel and all the nations.

---

[8] For other New Testament allusions to the Abrahamic blessing of the nations, cf. Acts 3:25–26; Ephesians 1:3; 1 Peter 3:9. On Paul's interpretation of the Abrahamic blessing of the nations, see J. M. Scott, *Paul and the Nations: The Old Testament and Jewish Background of Paul's Mission to the Nations with*

Blessing is a rich biblical notion that has been rather neglected in Christian theology. Blessing in the Bible refers to God's characteristically generous and abundant giving of all good to his creatures and his continual renewal of the abundance of created life. Blessing is God's provision for human flourishing. But it is also relational:[9] to be blessed by God is not only to know God's good gifts but to know God himself in his generous giving. Because it is relational the movement of blessing is a movement that goes out from God and returns to him. God's blessing of people overflows in their blessing of others and those who experience blessing from God in turn bless God, which means that they give all that creatures really can give to God: thanksgiving and praise.

Blessing highlights the relationship between creation and salvation in a different way from other ways of characterizing God's activity in the world. Already on the fifth day of the creation God blesses (Genesis 1:22). Blessing is the way God enables his creation to be fertile and fruitful, to grow and to flourish. It is in the most comprehensive sense God's purpose for his creation. Wherever human life enjoys the good things of creation and produces the good fruits of human activity, God is pouring out his blessing. Wherever people bless God for his blessings, to that extent God is known as the good Creator who provides for human flourishing. God's blessing is universal. But it is not the case that blessing is God's goodness in creation as distinct from his goodness in salvation, as has sometimes been proposed.[10] We could

---

[8] (*continued*) Special Reference to the Destination of Galatians (WUNT 84; Tübingen: Mohr [Siebeck] 1995), pp. 128–30.

[9] K. H. Richards, 'Bless/Blessing' in D. N. Freedman (ed.), *The Anchor Bible Dictionary* (New York: Doubleday, 1992), vol. 1, p. 754.

[10] Such a distinction was argued by C. Westermann, *Blessing in the Bible and the Life of the Church*, K. Crim (tr.) (Philadelphia: Fortress, 1978), but against it see Scharbert, 'brk', pp. 305–6.

not then make sense of the movement of blessing from Abraham to the nations that we have traced. Salvation too is God's blessing, since salvation is the fulfilment of God's good purposes for his creation, purposes already expressed in creation. But salvation is the fulfilment of God's purposes in spite of the damage evil does to God's creation. The Abrahamic blessing is more than the blessing of creation because it is designed to contend with and to overcome its opposite: God's curse.

With sin God's curse enters creation alongside God's blessing. We found the universal background to God's promise to Abraham in the account of the nations in Genesis 10–11. But there is an even earlier background in Genesis 3 and 4, where the blessings of creation turn to curse (3:17; 4:11). The curse even enters into God's promise to Abraham, apparently paralleling the blessing. God says to Abraham in Genesis 12: 'I will bless those who bless you, and the one who curses you I will curse' (Genesis 12:3; cf. 27:29; Numbers 24:9). But blessing predominates in the promise (as the difference between the plural 'those who bless you' and the singular 'the one who curses you' seems to suggest), and it is clearly blessing, not curse, that is the goal of God's calling of Abraham. Therefore blessing has the last word in the promise: 'in you all the families of the earth shall be blessed'.

Through the story of Israel curse continually accompanies blessing (e.g. Deuteronomy 7:12–16; 27–28), but the ultimate goal of God's promise to Abraham is the blessing that will prevail over the curse. It does so when the seed of Abraham, the singled-out descendant of Abraham, the Messiah, becomes 'a curse for us … so that in Christ Jesus the blessing of Abraham might come to the Gentiles' (Galatians 3:13–14). It is in this light that Paul can call the promise to Abraham that the nations will be blessed the gospel (Galatians 3:8). The secret of the promise is the bearing of the curse so that the blessing may prevail. The gospel is that in Jesus Christ the curse has been set aside and God's creative purpose for the blessing of his creation is established beyond any possibility of reversal. God's last and effective word is his blessing. It is a particular word, spoken in the life, death and resurrection of Jesus, broadcast by those who like Paul cannot but pass it on, so powerful is its effect, overflowing with blessing from those who, blessed by it, become a blessing to others.

2. From Israel to all the nations

If the book of Genesis singles out Abraham, the book of Exodus singles out Israel, the great nation promised to Abraham, the unique nation God creates to be his own. The first words God speaks to the people at Sinai are:

> You have seen what I did to the Egyptians, and how I bore you on eagles' wings and brought you to myself. Now therefore, if you obey my voice and keep my covenant, you shall be my treasured possession out of all the peoples. Indeed, the whole earth is mine, but you shall be for me a priestly kingdom and a holy nation.
>
> (Exodus 19:4–6a, NRSV)

All the nations – the whole earth – belong to YHWH, but he singles out Israel as his *special* possession. (The term 'treasured possession' [סגלה] indicates a king's personal treasure [cf. 1 Chronicles 29:3], distinguished from his ownership of his whole realm.) However, this very singularity of Israel is itself a witness to the nations. In his mighty acts of salvation for his own people God makes himself known to the other nations. God makes himself known *as* the God of Israel, in the particular identity he has given himself in choosing this one people as his own, but his acts on his people's behalf make him known at the same time as the one true God of all the earth, whom the nations themselves must also acknowledge. *This* narrative line from the one to the many, from the particular to the universal, is not necessarily about blessing. The nations are not always blessed. This trajectory is fundamentally about the knowledge of who God is, YHWH's demonstration of his deity to the nations.

In particular, YHWH delivered Israel from Egypt at the exodus, with acts of awesome power, in order, as the Hebrew Bible often says, to make his name renowned through all the earth, to make an enduring name for himself among the nations (Exodus 9:16; 2 Samuel 7:23; Nehemiah 9:10; Psalm 106:8; Isaiah 63:10, 12; Jeremiah 32:20; Daniel 9:15). We may have difficulty with this picture of God desiring and achieving fame for himself, something we would regard as self-seeking vanity and ambition if it were said of a human being. But this is surely one of those human analogies which is actually appropriate uniquely to God. For a human being to seek such universal and eternal fame would be to aspire to divinity, but God must desire to be known to be God. The good of God's human creatures requires that he be known to them as God. There is no vanity, only revelation of truth, in God's demonstrating of his deity to the nations.

The exodus, then, establishes a paradigmatic link between God's particular identity as the God of Israel and God's purpose of universal self-revelation to the nations.[11] This pattern of acts of salvation *for Israel* that make God known *to all the nations* recurs in later

---

[11] Here the non-Israelite Jethro's acknowledgement of YHWH as 'greater than all gods, because he delivered the people from the Egyptians' (Exodus 18:11) is exemplary.

instances: YHWH dried up the Jordan for Israel to cross 'so that all the peoples of the earth may know that the hand of the LORD is mighty' (Joshua 4:24); Hezekiah prays for deliverance from the Assyrian army 'so that all the kingdoms of the earth may know that you, LORD, are God alone' (1 Kings 19:19; Isaiah 37:20); Ezekiel prophesies God's restoration of Israel after exile, not for Israel's sake, but for the sake of God's name, so that 'the nations may know that he is the LORD' (Ezekiel 36:22–23; cf. 36:38; 38:23; 39:7).[12] Such knowledge is not necessarily of benefit to the nations. Ezekiel also regularly uses the formula 'they shall know that I am the LORD'[13] to express the effect of God's destructive judgements on the nations (e.g. 25:7, 11, 17; 26:6; 30:19, 25–26), as well as his acts of deliverance for Israel. The nations come to recognize Israel's God as the one who has power over all nations. But it is not at all clear that this acknowledgement of YHWH by the nations is beneficial to them.

In other instances there is a much more positive note. In part of Solomon's great prayer at the dedication of the Temple he imagines a non-Israelite from a distant land coming to Jerusalem because they have heard of YHWH's great name and his mighty acts. Solomon asks God to answer such a person's prayer 'so that all the peoples of the earth may know your name and fear you, as do your people Israel' (1 Kings 8:41–43; 2 Chronicles 6:32–33). This is glad acknowledgement of YHWH in reverence and worship stemming in the first place from knowledge of what he has done for his own people and spreading to all the nations. A similar sequence informs a number of the psalms that speak of the worship of God by all the nations:

---

[12] Cf. also 1 Samuel 17:46; 2 Kings 5:15.
[13] On Ezekiel's use of this formula, see Bailey Wells, *God's Holy People*, pp. 170–84.

May God be gracious to us and bless us
   and make his face to shine upon us,
   that your way may be known upon earth,
   your saving power among all nations.
Let the peoples praise you, O God;
   let all the peoples praise you
                  (Psalm 67:1–3, NRSV; cf. 22:21–27).

It is in this tradition that the later chapters of Isaiah
envisage the new exodus, the return of YHWH to Zion, as
an act of salvation that will demonstrate his deity to the
whole world: 'The LORD has bared his holy arm before
the eyes of all the nations; and all the ends of the earth
shall see the salvation of our God' (Isaiah 52:10, NRSV).
Deutero-Isaiah's prophecies about the great trial of truth
in which finally and decisively YHWH will make himself
known to all the nations as the only true God, the only
eternal one, the Creator of all things and Sovereign of all
history, the Saviour of Israel, are so theocentric that we
might think that, as with the first exodus, the point is no
more than the nations' acknowledgement of God in cra-
ven fear. But there is certainly more than that at stake.
YHWH makes himself known as the Saviour of Israel
who can also save all who turn to him. Israel are his witnesses to the nations that he is the only Saviour
(43:10–12). To the Gentiles ('the survivors of the
nations') who heed the witness, who recognize in Israel's
salvation that Israel's God can save whereas their idols
cannot, Israel's God issues the invitation:

Turn to me and be saved,
   all the ends of the earth!
For I am God, and there is no other.
By myself I have sworn,
   from my mouth has gone forth in righteousness a word

that shall not return:
'To me every knee shall bow, every tongue shall swear.'

(Isaiah 45:22–23, NRSV)

In this way God's new act of salvation for his unique people will prove to be also salvation for all the peoples.

It would be difficult to exaggerate the importance of the later chapters of Isaiah (40–66) for the first Christians and for the New Testament. It was these prophecies above all that gave early Christians the categories with which to interpret the history of Jesus and its consequences in the present and future. The commissioning of the apostles to be witnesses to the ends of the earth (Acts 1:8; 13:47) echoes Isaiah 49:6 (quoted in Acts 13:47). The new exodus prophesied in Isaiah, that definitive event of salvation in which YHWH will demonstrate his deity to the nations, took place – the early Christians recognized – in the life, death and resurrection of Jesus. It is in the crucified and risen Jesus that God makes himself known as the Saviour of Israel and the Saviour of the nations. The theocentric emphasis of this thematic trajectory[14] in the Old Testament and especially in Isaiah – that this is the way YHWH makes himself known to the world – can remind us that the mission to the nations in the New Testament also is directed to their acknowledgement and worship of the true God (1 Thessalonians 1:9; Acts 17:23–29; Revelation 14:7; 15:4) even before it is directed to the salvation that accompanies this. Its goal is the day when (in Paul's expansion of the words just quoted from Isaiah 45):

---

[14] Cf., on Ezekiel, ibid., p. 183: 'The overall purpose of everything YHWH does is that people should come to know that "I am YHWH."'

at the name of Jesus every knee should bend,
in heaven and on earth and under the earth,
and every tongue confess that Jesus Christ is Lord
to the glory of God the Father.

(Philippians 2:10, NRSV)

3. The king who rules from Zion to the ends of the earth

Just as YHWH singled out the one person Abraham and the one nation Israel, so he also singled out one place. From all the places of the world and all the places of the land of Israel, God selected one place as his own dwelling, 'to put his name there' as Deuteronomy has it (Deuteronomy 12:5; cf. 1 Kings 8:16, 29). This is mount Zion. The geographical specificity involved here – not merely of the land of Israel where God's people live, but also of mount Zion, where God lives in the midst of his people – is of indispensable significance in the Old Testament. More than God's presence with his own people, Zion is also the seat of God's universal rule. The cherubim in the holy of holies of Solomon's Temple constitute his throne, a kind of earthly equivalent of his throne in heaven. Many of the psalms celebrate this theme, for example:

The LORD is king; let the peoples tremble!
He sits enthroned upon the cherubim; let the earth quake!
The LORD is great in Zion;
    he is exalted over all the peoples.
Let them praise your great and awesome name.
Holy is he!

(Psalm 99:1–3, NRSV)

Here is God's universal kingdom *centred* in the particularity of mount Zion. (We shall return to this idea of
geographical centrality in the next chapter.)

But along with Zion, YHWH also *singled out* David
and installed him and his descendants as rulers in Jerusalem (cf. Psalm 78:67–71; 1 Kings 8:16). It is important to
note that the Old Testament is highly ambivalent about
earthly kings. On the one hand, YHWH alone is Israel's
king, and the establishment of monarchy in Israel was no
more than a divine concession to Israel's foolish desire to
be like the other nations. This was foolish because power
corrupts and kingship tends to tyranny and oppression.
Monarchy is certainly not portrayed as an ideal political
arrangement in the Old Testament. But on the other
hand, the Davidic king, adopted as God's son, rules on
God's behalf, as God's earthly deputy or vice-regent. As
the ideal human representative of God's own rule, this
human king's rule enacts God's justice and gives the
oppressed their rights. The modelling of earthly kingship
on God's creates a tension, even a contradiction, between
the ideal and the actual. We can see this in the Old Testament prophets' often severe criticisms of the kings of
Israel and Judah. There is no glossing over of the actual
failings and crimes of the kings who ruled God's people.
But we can also see the tension between the actual and
the ideal of monarchy in the prophetic hope, eventually
the messianic hope, for a truly ideal ruler in the future, a
king after God's own heart, a new David who will truly
embody God's own rule. This hope of a worthy human
representative of God's rule grew precisely as the inade-
quacies of actual monarchy were experienced by the
people and exposed by the prophets.

When the king is understood to rule as God's representative on earth, another kind of tension also arises – a
geographical one. YHWH's rule is universal, but the

Davidic king's, factually speaking, was not. Even David did not, of course, rule all the nations, though he and Solomon ruled a more extensive empire than was ever repeated in Israelite history. Consequently perhaps, few of the prophecies of a future king, an ideal David, seem to refer at all clearly to a more extensive rule than David's and Solomon's. The Messiah will, of course, be a force to be reckoned with on the international scene, as David and Solomon were, but will his empire be universal? Four closely connected passages deserve our attention.

The first is Psalm 72, whose title refers to Solomon and which is clearly a thoroughly ideal picture of the Davidic ruler. When this psalm is read within the whole canon of Scripture, the sheer hyperbole of what it says about the king invites a messianic interpretation.[15] Of the extent of his rule this is said:

> May he have dominion from sea to sea,
>   and from the River to the ends of the earth.
> May his foes bow down before him,
>   and his enemies lick the dust.
> May the kings of Tarshish and the isles render him tribute,
>   may the kings of Sheba and Seba bring gifts.
> May all kings fall down before him,
>   all nations give him service.
>
> (72:8–11, NRSV)

All this, like the whole psalm, is a prayer: not a statement of fact, but a prayer one would expect to be fulfilled in the messianic king. The first verse resembles a traditional

---

[15] Cf. K. M. Hein, 'The Perfect King of Psalm 72: An Intertextual Enquiry' in P. E. Satterthwaite, R. S. Hess and G. J. Wenham (eds), *The Lord's Anointed: Interpretation of Old Testament Messianic Texts* (Carlisle/Grand Rapids, Michigan: Paternoster/Baker, 1995), pp. 223–48.

description of the promised land, which stretches from the Red Sea to the Mediterranean and from the Euphrates river to the Negev desert (Exodus 23:31). Psalm 72:8 can be read in the same way except that 'the ends of the earth' replace the Negev. That this should be taken seriously would seem to follow from the fact that verse 10 goes on to refer to client kings at precisely the western and southern ends of the earth (Tarshish and the isles to the west, Sheba and Seba to the south). It seems as though the traditional limits of Israel's land have been opened up to universal scope. This king of Israel will not, in this picture, replace the kings of the nations, but they will acknowledge his overlordship, becoming the kind of client or subject kings that were attached to all the great ancient empires.

With this passage we can compare Zechariah 9:10, where the messianic king who 'shall command peace to the nations' is given precisely the same geographically described kingdom: 'His dominion shall be from sea to sea, and from the River to the ends of the earth' (9:10b, NRSV).

Similarly Micah 5:4 says of the future king of Israel, who is to come like a new David once again from Bethlehem, that Israel will live in security because 'he shall be great to the ends of the earth' (Micah 5:4; cf. also 7:12). These passages have in common an emphasis on peace as the longed-for characteristic of the future king's rule (cf. also Isaiah 9:6–7). He secures peace, it seems, by his international authority that encompasses all the nations to the limits of the world.

Much more bellicose is the rule of the king in Psalm 2, who must conquer the rebellious nations in order to implement the rule God gives him in the words: 'I will make the nations your heritage, and the ends of the earth your possession' (Psalm 2:8). But also here it is manifest that the human king exercises God's universal rule. He is enthroned on Zion and declared God's son (vv. 6–7). It is God who gives him God's own divine entitlement to rule the nations as well as Israel. Probably in part because this psalm so closely identifies the ideal king's rule with God's, as well as because of its emphatic universalism, it is frequently cited in the New Testament with reference to Jesus.

We noted the fundamental tension between the two Old Testament lines of thought about monarchy: that only YHWH is king and Israel should neither need nor want a human king, while on the other hand Israel's king rules as God's son on earth, dispensing God's justice. This tension is resolved in the messianic fulfilment as the New Testament portrays it. Earthly empire is subsumed once more into God's but in such a way that the human brotherliness of Israel's kings (cf. Deuteronomy 17:15, 20) is also assumed into God's universal rule. In the exaltation of Jesus to share God's own cosmic throne in heaven, the 'divinity' of the Davidic kings – the quasi-divinity they exercise as God's deputies – is reclaimed for God himself, but the humble solidarity of the ideal human king with his fellow-humans is also established on a cosmic scale. Human tyranny and divine distance are both ruled out by this christological form of the universal kingdom of God. Jesus is the one who rules in absolute, sovereign solidarity with God and in absolute, humble solidarity with his human sisters and brothers.

The geographical specificity and centrality of mount Zion, as we shall see in more detail in the next chapter, lose their significance for salvation history in the New Testament. Put another way, the literal geography of mount Zion, already laden with vast theological meaning in the Hebrew Bible, becomes an exclusively theological kind of geography in the New Testament (Hebrews

12:22; 2 Peter 1:18; Revelation 15:1; 21:10; cf. Galatians 4:26). Put yet another way, when in the last days, according to the prophets (Isaiah 2:2; Micah 4:1), the mountain of YHWH's house is raised above all other mountains, it is taken up into its heavenly archetype, the cosmic throne of God. But, if geographical specificity is transcended, the particular is not, for it is the man Jesus of Nazareth who rules from God's heavenly throne. In Jesus God's kingdom is both particular and universal, and mission is the mediation of the two. At the very end of the Acts of the Apostles, Luke leaves Paul in Rome 'proclaiming the kingdom of God and teaching about the Lord Jesus the Messiah' (Acts 28:31).

We have looked at three historic forms of the Bible's narrative movement from the particular to the universal. In each case we have started with an Old Testament particular. We have noted the singularity of God's choice as he singles out the one person Abraham, the one nation Israel, the one king David and the one place Zion. We have also seen how God's purpose always begins with such singling out but never ends there. It was never God's intention to bless Abraham purely for his and his descendants' sake. It was never God's intention to reveal himself to Israel only for Israel's sake. It was never God's intention to base his kingdom in Zion only so that he might rule the immediate locality. God's purpose in each of these singular choices was universal: that the blessing of Abraham might overflow to all the families of the earth, that God's self-revelation to Israel might make God known to all the nations, that from Zion his rule might extend to the ends of the earth. None of these forms of the biblical movement from the particular to the universal is, strictly speaking, mission. Abraham, Israel and David are not sent out to evangelize the world. But these three major trends of the biblical story are what make the church's mission intelligible as a necessary and coherent part of the whole biblical metanarrative. They establish the movement from the particular to the universal that the church is called in its mission to embody in a particular form. They establish the purpose of God for the world that, again, the church is called to serve in mission to the world. This is why we have been able, even if rather briefly, to trace the echoes of each of these Old Testament trajectories within the New Testament.

So it is in fact correct to say, as those who write about the biblical theology of mission have sometimes insisted, that the concept of mission itself is scarcely to be found in the Old Testament, but it is also essential to add that this does not diminish the importance of the Old Testament for the theme of Christian mission. Without these thematic trajectories from the Old Testament we could not understand the universal direction and goal that are everywhere apparent in the New Testament writings. It is not at all the case that the early Christians had to break out of the narrow particularism of their Jewish heritage in order to make Christianity a universal religion, as many people still seem to think. For in Old Testament theology the particular and the universal are not mutually exclusive or contradictory. The movement of God's purpose always starts from the particular on its way to the universal. God always singles out some for the sake of all. The early Christians, embarking on their mission to Gentiles as well as Jews, were carrying forward the universal purpose God established precisely when he chose Abraham, Israel, David and Zion.[16]

---

[16] J. LaGrand, *The Earliest Christian Mission to 'All Nations' in the Light of Matthew's Gospel* (Grand Rapids, Michigan: Eerdmans, 1995) shows well how in Matthew's Gospel there is no contradiction or even tension between Jesus' own mission to Israel alone and the church's universal mission to all nations,

There is also a quite essential and central element in that continuity between Old and New Testaments that I have, quite artificially, left out of that account. This is the particularity of Jesus himself. God's purposes could not in fact move directly from those he singled out in Old Testament times to the universal goal of his purposes. They had to be focused definitively in one more particular act of singling out an individual: Jesus the Jew from Nazareth. Jesus, in a sense, repeats the particularity of each of the three chosen ones we have studied. He is the descendant of Abraham through whom all the families of the earth will be blessed. He assumes for himself his nation Israel's own destiny to be a light to all the nations (Luke 2:31–32). He is the new, the ideal, David, the only one truly able to be the human embodiment of God's rule over all. But when we see Jesus' particularity in these ways, in the categories established by the Old Testament, then we at once see also his universality. We can see how it makes sense that the New Testament is amazingly focused on this particular human person, who dominates its every page, while at the same time it constantly speaks the language of universal truth, universal relevance and universal effect. The whole of New Testament thought is unified around the universal relevance of precisely the particular human being Jesus.

Therefore the church which recognized Jesus in those terms and still recognizes Jesus in those terms is called to universal witness to Jesus. As the followers of this

---

[16] (*continued*) since Israel's role in God's purposes was to be a light to the nations. 'Jesus' ministry to Israel related to Israel's indispensable role in the mission to the nations. So it is that the most "particularistic" words and deeds of Jesus are the most promising to the nations' (pp. 205–6). The Twelve 'were prepared as God's agents ... for *Israel's mission to the nations*' (p. 251, italics original).

particular man, as themselves called and chosen by God as the church of Jesus Christ, as the particular community the church is in any specific time and place, the church is always caught up in the movement of God's purpose from one to all. God never singles out some for their own sake alone, but always for others. So the church should be the community from which the blessing of Abraham, experienced in Jesus, overflows to others. The church should be the people who have recognized God as he truly is in God's revelation in Jesus and therefore make that revelation known to others. The church is those people who, so far, acknowledge God's rule as he is implementing it in Jesus and live for others in the light of the coming of his kingdom in all creation.

We come to the fourth and last of our thematic forms of the biblical movement from the particular to the universal. This one stands somewhat apart from the others because it is not so much another narrative movement to be placed alongside the other three, but rather a movement that characterizes all of those three, as well as the mission of the church. This is the movement to all by way of the least.

4. To all by way of the least

In this case we shall begin in the New Testament. Paul writes to his converts in Corinth, evidently a highly status-conscious group of people:

> Not many of you were wise by human standards, not many were powerful, not many were of noble birth. But God chose what is foolish in the world to shame the wise; God chose what is weak in the world to shame the strong; God chose what is low and despised in the world, things

that are not, to reduce to nothing things that are, so that
no one may boast in the presence of God.

(1 Corinthians 1:26b–29, NRSV)

Recent studies on 1 Corinthians[17] have made very clear
that social status is the issue in much of Paul's debate
with the dominant faction in the Corinthian church. The
people Paul calls the wise are those skilled in rhetoric,
able to make clever and impressive speeches, while the
foolish are the uneducated. Rhetoric was a major means
of social advancement, and so the wise are also
the powerful élite, or those who aspire to join them. The
strong are those whose wealth and social position give
them power and influence in society, while the people
Paul calls weak are the powerless, the ordinary people
with no say and no muscle in this social world. At
Corinth – and Paul certainly does not mean only at
Corinth – God *singled out* the poor and the powerless,
choosing to begin his work with them, not because God's
love does not extend to the cultural and social élite, but
actually for the sake of the wealthy and the powerful as
well as for the poor and the humble. God's love has to
reach the strong via the weak, because the strong can
receive the love of God only by abandoning their pretensions to status above others. Only when they see in
God's choice of those without status that status counts
for nothing in God's sight can they abandon the
arrogance and the vested interests that prevent their right

---

[17] E.g. S. M. Pogoloff, *Logos and Sophia: The Rhetorical Situa-
tion of 1 Corinthians* (SBLDS 134; Atlanta, Georgia: Scholars
Press, 1992); R. Pickett, *The Cross in Corinth: The Social
Significance of the Death of Jesus* (JSNTSS 143; Sheffield:
Sheffield Academic Press, 1997); G. Tomlin, *The Power of the
Cross: Theology and the Death of Christ in Paul, Luther and
Pascal* (Carlisle: Paternoster, 1999), Part 1.

relationship both with God and with others. God's 'shaming' of the wise and the strong, in Paul's words, is this redemptive contradiction of their values.

In this passage and its context Paul does something rather remarkable. In the first place, by echoing the Old Testament, he identifies a consistent divine strategy, a characteristic way in which God works, to which the origins of the church at Corinth conform. The God who chose the first Corinthian converts is the God who chose the least significant of all the peoples (Israel) for his own (Deuteronomy 7:7). This is Hannah's God, who exalts the lowly and humbles the exalted (1 Samuel 2:3–8), just as he is also Mary's God, who fills the hungry and dismisses the rich (Luke 1:51–53). This is the God who chose the youngest of Jesse's sons, David, the one no one had even thought to summon (1 Samuel 16:6–13). This is the God who habitually overturns status, not in order to make the non-élite a new élite, but in order to abolish status, to establish his kingdom in which none can claim privilege over others and all gladly surrender privilege for the good of others. We could trace the theme also through the gospel teaching and actions of Jesus. Modern writers have often spoken of Jesus' option for the marginalized – a better term than 'poor' (used without explanation) since they include people not lacking in material goods but marginal in other ways. 'Marginal' or 'socially excluded' are effective modern metaphors, but the Bible itself does not seem to use metaphors of horizontal direction in this way. Its usual metaphors are of vertical direction, of high and low status. God raises the lowly and brings down the exalted. God himself not only inhabits the highest heaven, but comes among the humblest of his servants on earth (cf. Isaiah 57:15).

Paul not only sees this as God's usual strategy in human affairs; he also recognizes it paradigmatically in the cross. The claim that God is to be encountered and salvation found in a crucified man – a man stripped of all status and honour, dehumanized, the lowest of the low – is the offence of the cross. This is the real scandal of particularity – not just that God's universal purpose pivots on one particular human being (though that was stumbling-block enough for the philosophically educated in Paul's day and the Enlightenment rationalists of our own), but, much worse, that God's universal purpose pivots on *this* particular human being, the crucified one. No wonder the rulers of this age did not recognize him (1 Corinthians 2:8). For those who see God in the image of their own power and status there could be no recognition of God in the cross. And yet the Christ who thus demeaned himself to the depths of human degradation, as Paul says in Philippians 2:6–11, is the one God has exalted to the throne of the universe so that every knee should bow and every tongue confess that he is Lord. The act of universal salvation of which the later prophecies of Isaiah spoke, the act which demonstrates God's deity to the nations, the new thing that God does for Israel so that the nations too may recognize him as Saviour – this is the exaltation of the crucified Christ. God defined his own kingdom when he exalted the crucified Christ.

So God's way to his universal kingdom is through a movement of identification with the least. Paul's own apostolic ministry of proclaiming the crucified Christ had also in some sense to conform to this movement of identification with the least.[18] This was his problem at

---

[18] On Paul's missionary practice as imitative of Christ's kenosis, see M. D. Hooker, 'A Partner in the Gospel: Paul's Understanding of His Ministry' in E. H. Lovering and J. L. Sumney (eds), *Theology and Ethics in Paul and his Interpreters: Essays in Honor of Victor Paul Furnish* (Nashville: Abingdon, 1996), pp. 83–100.

Corinth. The Corinthians wanted Paul to behave like an eminent travelling philosopher, to accept the hospitality of the wealthiest among them, to display the status-enhancing rhetoric of cultured people. They wanted to enhance their own status by basking in the reflected glory of his. Instead Paul conformed his manner to his message, rejecting the orator's ability to sway the audience by adapting his message to their taste. The power of the cross lay in its offence to their taste. At the same time Paul financed himself by hard manual work that demeaned him to the level of the slave. He embarrassed his upwardly mobile converts. But he reached the ordinary people, mixing with them on their own level in his friends' leather-working shop. His missionary policy of becoming all things to all people was weighted in the direction of the poor. 'To the weak', he says, 'I became weak, that I might win the weak' (1 Corinthians 9:22), but not that to the strong he became strong. Of course, Paul did not hold aloof from the privileged, any more than Jesus did, and he would claim his own privilege as a Roman citizen when it suited his purpose. But the power-ful people and the upwardly mobile people had to take Paul as they found him, just as they had to take the cruci-fied Christ as God's radical contradiction of their values.

This fourth of our thematic trajectories through the biblical story is a necessary reminder that the church's mission cannot be indifferent to the inequalities and injustices of the world into which it is sent. The gospel does not come to each person only in terms of some abstracted generality of human nature, but in the realities and differences of their social and economic situations. It engages with the injustices of the world on its way to the kingdom of God. This means that as well as the out-ward movement of the church's mission in geographical extension and numerical increase, there must also be this (in the Bible's imagery) downward movement of solidarity with the people at the bottom of the social scale of importance and wealth. It is to these – the poorest, those with no power or influence, the wretched, the neglected – to whom God has given priority in the kingdom, not only for their own sake, but also for all the rest of us who can enter the kingdom only alongside *them*.

Chapter 3

Geography – Sacred and Symbolic

Biblical scholars and theologians have usually found biblical history more significant than biblical geography. Yet there is a great deal of geography in the Bible, much of it literal, but much of it also used with symbolic significance. (We cannot usually appreciate geographical symbolism without first understanding the literal reference of the geographical terms that are used symbolically.) Moreover, geography is a massively important feature of people's experience of life. It is a key ingredient in the particularity of human experience. The places where we live affect who we are, and to a large extent it has been geography that has made possible the rich diversity of human cultures and societies that globalization now threatens. The church's own history has been significantly shaped by geography. Of special interest for us now is the fact that the gospel has so often impelled Christians to cross geographical boundaries and to journey to unknown places in obedience to the direction from the particular to the universal that the Bible points.

1. Geographical horizon and representative geography

What kind of awareness of the world of the nations does the Bible have? What are its geographical horizons?

The best place to start is with the table of the nations in Genesis 10. When, from Genesis 12 onwards, readers of Scripture learn that the purpose of God through Abraham and his descendants is to bless all the families of the earth or all the nations, the natural referent for those phrases is the account of all the nations of the world, tabulated as a great genealogy of the descendants of Noah, in Genesis 10. This is the known world from Israel's perspective in the Old Testament period. Not all of the names can be identified with complete confidence, but most of them can, and the geographical limits of this world are relatively clear. To the west it extends to the western end of the Mediterranean (Tarshish).[1] To the south Cush (Ethiopia) reaches from Upper Egypt to an undefined extent through modern Sudan into modern Ethiopia.[2] To the north Gomer and Ashkenaz – the Cimmerians and the Scythians – inhabit an equally undefined area stretching north from the Caucasus and the Black Sea. To the east, Elam is the area of south-western Iran immediately east of Mesopotamia. Only in this last direction is the Old Testament's geographical horizon further extended elsewhere within the Hebrew Bible. In the sixth century the Persian Empire opened up the previously scarcely known east, for Israel as it did also at

---

[1] Jonah flees to Tarshish (Jonah 1:3) because it is the western end of the earth, the furthest point he can reach from Israel at most speed (travel by sea was quicker than travel by land).

[2] Hazarmaveth (Genesis 10:26), i.e. Hadramaut, lies at roughly the same latitude in the south of Arabia. If Put (Genesis 10:6) were correctly identified as the place the Egyptians knew as Punt, probably Somalia, it would be even further south, but it is more probably Libya: see J. Simons, 'The "Table of Nations" (Genesis 10): Its General Structure and Meaning' in R. S. Hess and D. T. Tsumura (eds), *'I Studied Inscriptions from before the Flood': Ancient Near Eastern, Literary, and Linguistic Approaches to Genesis 1–11* (Sources for Biblical and Theological Study 4; Winona Lake, Indiana: Eisenbrauns, 1994), pp. 250–53.

the same time for the Greeks. Most dramatically, the narrative of the book of Esther takes place in the Persian imperial capital, Susa, located in Elam on the far eastern limit of the world of Genesis 10. But Susa was the capital and centre of an empire that stretched as far east – to India – as it did west – to Egypt and Ethiopia (Esther 1:1; 8:9).[3] Esther is the only biblical book to refer to India[4] or to anywhere so far to the east.

Genesis 10's omission not only of India but also of the Persians,[5] so important for the latest part of the Old Testament story, shows that it is a historically particular view of the extent of the world, even though its particularity corresponds to that of most of the Old Testament. It is in fact impressively comprehensive. There are not many peoples mentioned elsewhere in the Old Testament who do not appear in it.[6] Later Jews adapted and reinterpreted the table, to take account of growing geographical knowledge, as well as the fact that the identity of many of the names was later forgotten.[7] But there is another way in which Genesis 10 is, as it were, *open to* changing

---

[3] According to Strabo (*Geography* 15.3.2), Cyrus the Persian, having conquered the Medes, realized that his native Persia was now on the edges of his empire and so moved his capital to the more central Susa.

[4] In the Apocrypha, see also 1 Maccabees 6:37.

[5] Unless Madai (Genesis 10:2), i.e. the Medes, includes them, as apparently in Isaiah 13:17; 21:2; Jeremiah 51:11, 28.

[6] Genesis 10 understandably omits nations which, in the perspective of Genesis, originated later: Moab, Ammon, Edom and Israel herself. The same may be true of peoples named among the descendants of Nahor (Genesis 22:21–22), Abraham and Keturah (25:2–4), and Ishmael (25:13–15), though some of the names in these genealogies also appear in Genesis 10. Other unmentioned peoples include Ararat (2 Kings 19:37; Jeremiah 51:27), and Minni (Jeremiah 51:27).

[7] For a survey of non-biblical Jewish interpretation of the table of the nations, see Scott, *Paul and the Nations*, pp. 14–56.

geographical perceptions and horizons. The number of
descendants of Shem, Ham and Japheth listed is precisely
seventy.

This is a significant number. It must be related to
the more common symbolism of the number seven in the
Bible, and probably suggests completeness. The number
seven in the Bible regularly indicates completeness, but it
can also designate a limited number that is intended to
stand, representatively, for all. The Fourth Evangelist
narrates seven of Jesus' 'signs' as representative of the
many others which, he tells us, Jesus did but he could
not record. The seven churches to which the book of
Revelation is addressed stand representatively for all the
churches that might also read the book. This kind of
representativeness does not abolish the particularity of
the seven actually named, as though they became mere
symbols. The seven churches in Revelation are quite
precisely characterized and addressed in terms quite
specific to their circumstances, but their very variety
enables them also to stand in for other churches which
would all be able to find some point of contact between
their own circumstances and those of these churches, seeing themselves perhaps in one or other of the seven. The
example of the seven churches in Revelation encouraged
Christians, in the period in which the New Testament
canon was being defined, to apply the same notion to
Paul's letters. The Pauline collection of letters to churches
is addressed to seven of Paul's churches; by writing to
seven specific churches, claims the Muratorian Canon,
Paul in fact addressed the whole church. It is unlikely to
be accidental that the New Testament canon includes not
only Pauline letters to seven churches, but also seven
so-called catholic letters.

Returning to geography and nations, we can see the
same principle of a list of seven serving to represent all in

some lists of seven nations in the Hebrew Bible. Ezekiel seems particularly fond of this device: chapters 25–32 present oracles against seven nations (Ammon, Moab, Edom, Philistines, Tyre, Sidon and Egypt), while Egypt then joins six other nations depicted as lying slain among the dead (Assyria, Elam, Meshech, Tubal, Edom, Sidonians).[8] In Ezekiel's strange oracle against Gog in chapter 38, an exotic list of seven nations comprise the army Gog leads against Israel: Meshech, Tubal, Persia, Ethiopia, Put (Libya), Gomer and Beth-togarmah. All of these are distant nations with whom Israel in her history had had few direct dealings. As the book of Revelation correctly interprets them, they are 'the nations at the four corners of the earth' (Revelation 20:8; cf. Isaiah 11:12). Probably the names follow a circle starting from Meshech and Tubal in the north, moving to Persia in the east, then to Ethiopia in the south, Libya in the west, and returning to Gomer and Beth-togarmah in the north.[9] But the specific seven are surely representative of all the distant nations. We shall return to these distant nations shortly.

The seventy nations of Genesis 10, then, are a representative list, its seventy quite specific actual nations standing for all nations on earth. It would, of course, be absurd to expect Genesis to name nations or places utterly unknown in Israel's world – Japan or New Zealand or even Britain – but the universal horizon projected by Genesis 10 and the rest of the canonical writings that presuppose it encompasses representatively all other

---

[8] Note also Egypt with six allies in 30:4–5.

[9] Some commentators attempt to place all these nations in the north, as Ezekiel 38:15; 39:2 might suggest (so D. I. Bock, *The Book of Ezekiel: Chapters 25–48* [NICOT; Grand Rapids, Michigan: Eerdmans, 1998], p. 439). But if we allow all the named nations their usual identity, Gog himself and the majority of his allies come from the north, while also being joined by allies from the other three points of the compass.

inhabited parts of the world. I call this representative geography. It is important to note that it does not turn the specific peoples and places mentioned into mere symbols. They retain their reality and their own real particularity, but they also stand representatively for all other places or peoples. This is one way in which we can understand the relationship of particularity and universality in biblical geography.

We can take this idea of representative geography a little further, in an interesting direction, by focusing on the nations at the ends of the earth. In the Bible the Ethiopians are one of these nations at the ends of the earth. The Old Testament refers rather frequently to the end or ends of the earth (there is not usually any distinction between the singular and the plural forms). It is one of the most vivid ways of making universal reference to the whole inhabited world, common especially in the Psalms and in the later chapters of Isaiah, where it evokes the universal sovereignty of YHWH, and the vindication, acknowledgement and worship of YHWH by even the most distant peoples.[10] A geographical movement that extends to the ends of the earth obviously encompasses all the nations between the centre and those edges of the world. Of course, the idea of edges of the earth implies some central position from which one measures distance outwards to the edges. Implicitly in the Old Testament it is Israel that is pictured as the centre of the inhabited world and the nations most distant from Palestine are placed at the edges of the world. In Psalm 72, which we considered in our previous chapter, the king's dominion 'to the ends of the earth' is specified by reference to the tribute brought by the kings of Tarshish and the isles (the far west) and the kings of Sheba and Seba (the far south)

---

[10] e.g. Psalm 22:27; 48:10; 59:13; 65:5; 67:7; 98:3; Isaiah 40:28;
41:5, 9; 43:6; 45:22; 48:20; 49:6; 52:10; 62:11; Jeremiah 16:19.

(72:10), just as the New Testament says that the Queen of the South, i.e. of Sheba, came from the ends of the earth to Solomon's court (Matthew 12:42). Clearly in the psalm these distant places at two of the cardinal directions from Israel are representative examples of the nations on the edges of Israel's world.

In prophecies of the time when all the nations will acknowledge the God of Israel and his people and come to worship in Jerusalem it is the nations to the south – Egypt, Ethiopia and others – who are most often specified in this representative role (Psalm 68:31 [Egypt, Ethiopia]; Isaiah 45:14 [Egypt, Ethiopia, Sabeans]; Zechariah 14:18–19 [Egypt]), perhaps because the exodus made Egypt Israel's archetypal enemy.[11] But specially worth our attention here are two cases where the prophets refer not merely to Ethiopia (Cush), that ill-defined area that bordered Upper Egypt in the north of modern Sudan, but more precisely to the far south, a land said to be divided by rivers and located 'beyond the rivers of Ethiopia' (Isaiah 18:1, 2, 7; Zephaniah 3:10). The rivers must be the White Nile, the Blue Nile and the Atbara.[12]

For the ancient Greeks, too, the Ethiopians were at the edge of the earth, designated 'the furthest of men' (ἐσχατοί ἀνδρῶν) by Homer,[13] but there is a rather significant contrast between the ways the Greeks and the prophets of Israel regarded the Ethiopians. For the Greeks the Ethiopians and the other peoples on the edges

[11] For a different explanation, see N. K. Gottwald, *All the Kingdoms of the Earth: Israelite Prophecy and International Relations in the Ancient Near East* (New York: Harper & Row, 1964), p. 223.

[12] E. Ullendorf, *Ethiopia and the Bible* (Schweich Lectures 1967; London: Oxford University Press for the British Academy, 1968), p. 6.

[13] J. S. Romm, *The Edges of the Earth in Ancient Thought* (Princeton: Princeton University Press, 1992), p. 49.

of the world were the stuff of mythology and tall tales: in Homer, for example, the Ethiopians are 'the blameless Ethiopians' uniquely visited by the gods who join their banquets. The Old Testament prophets, on the other hand, are quite factual. The Ethiopians are 'tall and smooth-skinned' and travel the Nile (or perhaps the Red Sea) on papyrus boats (Isaiah 18:2, 7), such as are still used on lake Tana in modern Ethiopia. This description in Isaiah 18 is no doubt factual because it reflects the visit of actual Ethiopians from the far south to Jerusalem as ambassadors (Isaiah 18:1–2). But it highlights the fact that the Old Testament never mythologizes the distant peoples as the Greeks habitually did. These nations at the edges of the earth are no more godlike and no more bestial than other people. They do not live longer than others, avoid sickness or thrive on exotic diets. They neither satisfy the common human appetite for travellers' tales of distant marvels nor serve as virtuous contrasts to civilized decadence. The distant peoples are simply ordinary peoples who, as it happens, live very far from the centre of the world, and with whom Israel therefore had only very occasional contact.

Here is Zephaniah's prophecy of the role of the Ethiopians of the far south in the eschatological future:

> At that time I will change the speech of the peoples to a
>   pure speech,
>   that all of them may call on the name of the LORD
>   and serve him with one accord.
> From beyond the rivers of Ethiopia
>   my suppliants, my scattered ones,
>   shall bring my offering.
>
> (3:9–10, NRSV)

These verses seem best understood as alluding to the story of the tower of Babel in Genesis 11, with which there are a number of striking verbal contacts.[14] Whereas the builders of the tower had been united in attempting to make a name for themselves (Genesis 11:4), the peoples in the future will be united in calling on the name of YHWH. In place of the 'confused' speech of the nations after Babel, there will be 'pure' speech. And the 'scattered ones', those whom YHWH had scattered abroad from Babel over the face of all the earth (Genesis 11:8), are now 'my scattered ones'[15] who are re-gathered as they bring their offerings to YHWH in his Temple in Jerusalem. Those from the deep south, from beyond the rivers of Ethiopia, therefore function here as representative of all the nations scattered over the whole earth. In Israel's world they were as far scattered as one could get.

This idea of representative geography is helpful in enabling us to read the universalism of Old Testament prophecy correctly. The prophets depict the universal future, the eschatological future that God's universal lordship entailed, in terms of the specific peoples of whom they knew in their world. These peoples do not lose their own particularity in becoming also representative. The eschatological future really is a future for all nations, these included. But their own particularity stands for the particularity also of every other people and place.

Our final example is the one that comes closest to the New Testament idea of mission to all the nations. Close to the end of the book of Isaiah God says:

---

[14] R. L. Smith, *Micah–Malachi* (WBC 32; Waco, Texas: Word, 1984), p. 142 recognizes the allusion to Genesis 11 but does not pay full attention to all the points of contact.

[15] Some commentators take these to be Jews resident in Ethiopia, but the connexion with v. 9 is then lost.

> I am coming to gather all nations and tongues;
> 　and they shall come and see my glory,
> 　and I will set a sign among them.
> From them I will send survivors to the nations,
> 　to Tarshish, Put [Libya], and Lud [Lydia],
> 　to Meshech,[16] Tubal and Javan [the Greeks],
> 　to the coastlands [or islands] far away
> 　that have not heard my fame or seen my glory;
> 　and they shall declare my glory among the nations.
> 　　　　　　　　　　(Isaiah 66:18–19, NRSV altered)

The passage is unique within the Hebrew Bible in speaking of people sent to the nations to declare God's glory to them. These are the distant nations, those who have not witnessed or heard more immediately of God's salvific acts for his people. If we count the nations mentioned and include the final, rather general reference to the coastlands or islands, the list comes to seven, the representative number.[17] They stand, then, for all the nations. Tarshish, Put [Libya], Meshech and Tubal represent the distant nations in other texts we have considered, but the list as a whole is very distinctive. These places seem all to be to the north and west: Meshech and Tubal are probably in the north-east of modern Turkey, Lud [Lydia] represents western and southern Turkey, Javan the Greeks of Ionia and Greece,

---

[16] This translation follows LXX rather than MT at this point; cf. R. Riesner, *Paul's Early Period*, D. Stott (tr.) (Grand Rapids, Michigan: Eerdmans, 1998), p. 252.

[17] There is a parallel but different list of nations from which the exiled Israelites will be regathered in Isaiah 11:11. In this case there are seven nations (Assyria, Egypt, Pathros, Ethiopia, Elam, Shinar [Babylon], Hamath) *excluding* the concluding reference to the coastlands or islands. Though the list corresponds to 'the four corners of the earth' (11:12), not many of the nations named are far distant nations (Ethiopia, Elam).

Put [Libya] perhaps the Mediterranean coast of Africa west of Egypt, and Tarshish the far west, most likely Spain. The coastlands or islands – the word (אִיִּים) is used of lands that one crossed the sea to reach[18] – are most naturally, after this list of names, those of the Mediterranean. This is in fact the world of the early Christian mission as depicted in Acts and Paul's letters. As some scholars have suggested, Paul may actually have taken this text as the geographical programme for his own missionary journeys (though he probably would not have identified all the places precisely as we do).[19] But Paul's missionary journeys were themselves only part of the early Christian mission, taking the gospel to one area of the known world, and recounted by Luke as representative, standing in for the rest of the story that he does not narrate.[20] The principle of geographical representativeness with reference to the universal purpose of God thus spills over from the Old into the New Testament.

2. The Centre and the Horizon

In Ezekiel 5:5 God says of Jerusalem: 'I have set her in the centre of the nations, with countries all around her' (cf. also 38:12). This picture of Jerusalem, more specifically mount Zion, as the centre of the known world, with the other nations imagined in concentric circles moving

---

[18] Cf. W. Horowitz, 'The Isles of the Nations: Genesis x and Babylonian Geography' in J. A. Emerton (ed.), *Studies in the Pentateuch* (VTSup 41; Leiden: Brill, 1990), pp. 35–43.

[19] Riesner, *Paul's Early Period*, pp. 245–53. Probably Paul, like Josephus (*Antiquities* 1.127), identified Tarshish with Tarsus. But, for criticism of Riesner's proposal, see Scott, *Paul and the Nations*, pp. 145–7.

[20] This should be clear from the geographical horizon for mission that Luke himself provides in Acts 2:5–11.

outwards from Israel towards the edges of the earth is, as we have noticed, implied in many parts of the Old Testament. It is also the picture presupposed in Jesus' commission to the apostles in Acts 1:8, where their mission of witness moves out from Jerusalem, initially to Judea and Samaria, finally to the ends of the earth, taking in all the nations on the way.

There is nothing very surprising about this biblical picture of the world having its centre in Jerusalem. It is not unusual, but rather common, for peoples to construct their mental world map with themselves at the centre and their own sacred place identified as the centre of the world. For the ancient Greeks Delphi was the 'navel' of the world.[21] But such a picture easily supports a kind of ethnocentrism that evaluates those at the centre as superior and treats distance from the centre as a measure of inferiority. The Greek historian Herodotus treats the Persians as representative of this view:

> They honor most the peoples nearest to themselves, next the people next to those, and others in proportion to their remoteness, and those dwelling furthest from themselves they hold in the least honor. (1.134)[22]

Herodotus himself, contemptuous of such a view, counters it with a kind of inverse ethnocentrism, in which the most distant peoples, those, like the Ethiopians, at the edges of the world, are idealized, held up as a virtuous contrast to the imperfect culture of the

---

[21] Ezekiel 38:12 may use the same metaphor.

[22] Quoted in Romm, *The Edges of the Earth in Ancient Thought*, p. 55. Cf. the Persian map of the world, with Persia at the centre and Ethiopia, Libya, Greece, Thrace and the Scythians around the edges, constructed from inscriptions of Darius I in P. Goukowsky, *Essai sur les Origines du Mythe d'Alexandre (336–270 AV. J.-C.)* (Nancy: University of Nancy II, 1978), vol. 1, p. 223.

central people, whoever they might be who think themselves such.

Israel – or at least the prophets of Israel – seems not
to have been concerned with the issues of cultural superiority and inferiority that inspired the Greeks' contempt
for barbarians. As we have seen, the distant peoples in the
Old Testament are neither idealized nor considered
barbaric. They are simply nations like all the others, and
the difference between Israel and all the nations lies only
in the undeserved election of Israel by YHWH to be his one
people for the sake of bringing blessing to all the peoples.
Israel is called to be faithful to her covenant with YHWH,
not for the sake of superiority but in order to model this
covenant relationship as an invitation to others. Israel's
ethnocentric temptation was to presume on her privilege,
and it is to refute that presumption that the prophet
Amos famously cut Israel down to the same size as the
other nations:

> Are you not like the Ethiopians to me,
> O people of Israel? says the LORD.
> Did I not bring Israel up from Egypt,
>   and the Philistines from Caphtor [probably Crete]
>   and the Aramaeans from Kir
>   [probably eastern Mesopotamia]?
>
> (Amos 9:7, NRSV)

Just as YHWH has brought some of Israel's national
neighbours also from distant parts of the earth, so he
could, if he chose, raise up another people for himself
from the ends of the earth and place them at the centre.[23]
The Ethiopians would do just as well as Israel. This is
not in the least a denial of Israel's election, which Amos
himself so strongly asserts: 'You only have I known of all

---

[23] A similar point is made by John the Baptist in Matthew 3:9;
Luke 3:8.

the families of the earth' (3:2). Rather it is an assertion of YHWH's sovereignty, his ability and right to choose whatever nation he pleases to be the special vehicle of his purpose for the world. Centrality is a matter of YHWH's choice alone. The most distant of nations, the Ethiopians, are by no means inferior.[24]

Greek ethocentricity – the routine contempt of the Greeks for all non-Greeks – is pointedly repudiated by Paul, who writes in Colossians that, in the renewed humanity, 'there is no longer Greek and Jew, circumcised and uncircumcised, barbarian, Scythian, slave, free: but Christ is all and in all' (3:11, NRSV altered). The mention of one specific people, the Scythians, who appear nowhere else in the New Testament, may seem surprising. But in Paul's world the Scythians correspond to the Ethiopians at the opposite point of the compass.[25] They are the distant peoples of the north, nomads of the steppes to the north of the Black Sea. Though idealized by some Greek writers, in line with the inverse ethnocentrism already mentioned, in the general view they were considered the most barbaric of barbarians, uncivilized savages.[26] Josephus the Jew (*Against Apion* 2.269), appropriating, like other hellenized people, the cultural

---

[24] Cf. Gottwald, *All the Kingdoms of the Earth*, p. 117: 'Amos succeeds in establishing both Israel's importance as a unique people and her merely proximate importance to a God for whom all peoples count and who possesses many resources for bringing justice to the earth.'

[25] G. L. Byron, *Symbolic Blackness and Ethnic Difference in Early Christian Literature* (London: Routledge, 2002), p. 33; D. Goldenberg, 'Scythian-Barbarian: The Permutations of a Classical Topos in Jewish and Christian Texts of Late Antiquity', *Journal of Jewish Studies* 49 (1998), pp. 91–4.

[26] The sophisticated art of Scythian metal work, now well known from archeology (see, e.g., T. Talbot Rice, *The Scythians* [London: Thames & Hudson, 1957]), must have been known to the Greeks, but could not counter-balance their notorious cruelty and indiscriminate killing of enemies.

superiority of the Greeks, calls the Scythians 'little better than wild animals'. Paul's is in fact the more authentically Jewish perspective, aligning Greeks with Scythians much as Amos aligned Israel with Ethiopians.

According to the usual understanding of Colossians 3:11, Paul mentions first the general category of 'barbarian', the Greek term for all non-Greeks, expressive of the Greek sense of superiority to all such non-Greeks, and then mentions the more specific category of 'Scythian', regarded as the most barbaric of barbarians. There is, however, a difficulty with this interpretation, because the other three pairs mentioned by Paul in this verse ('Greek and Jew, circumcised and uncircumcised ... slave, free') are antitheses. The pair 'barbarian, Scythian' as usually understood would not fit this pattern. But David Goldenberg has made the attractive suggestion that 'barbarian' (βάρβαρος) here refers to the people who live at the southern end of the earth, so that 'barbarian, Scythian' refers to the nations at the southern and northern extremes. It is a geographical or racial (black races/ white races) contrast, paralleling the national (Greek and Jew), religious (circumcised and uncircumcised), and social ('slave, free') contrasts in the rest of Paul's list. Goldenberg refers to the term Barbaria as a place name for an area of East Africa (Sudan, Eritrea, Somalia), and to the fact that when rabbinic literature makes use of the standard pairing of Ethiopians and Scythians, as the peoples of the southern and northern extremes of the world, the term 'barbarians' (ברברים) appears instead of Ethiopians.[27] If this is a correct interpretation of Colossians 3:11, Paul is referring not only to the universal

---

[27] Goldenberg, 'Scythian-Barbarian', pp. 87–102; for the names Barbaria and Barbarian, see also D. Goldenberg, 'Geographia Rabbinica: The Toponym Barbaria', *Journal of Jewish Studies* 50 (1999), pp. 53–73.

scope of the gospel's inclusiveness (from extreme south to extreme north) but also to the transcendence of racial differences and divisions in Christ.

When reading the Old Testament narratives, it is easy to lose sight of Israel's destiny to be a blessing to the nations, and we depend on the canonical framework given to Israel's story by Genesis and some of the prophets to see it that way. But what is constantly brought to our attention is Israel's place among the nations. Israel's story is certainly not one of parochial isolation, and it is indeed Israel's geographical location, what Ezekiel calls her centrality among the nations, that makes it clear that her destiny is bound up with that of the nations: her immediate neighbours, the great empires to whose power she succumbs, and even the more distant nations whom these empires bring into Israel's view and occasionally into actual contact with Israel. Whether it is because people 'from all the nations' came to hear the wisdom of Solomon (1 Kings 4:34; cf. 4:31; 10:24) or because king Hezekiah was 'exalted in the sight of all nations' (2 Chronicles 32:23) or because Israel is scattered in exile 'among all peoples, from one end of the earth to the other' (Deuteronomy 28:64), the universal horizon remains inescapable throughout Israel's story. Significant episodes in Israel's own story take place as far from the land of Israel as Upper Egypt (Pathros: Jeremiah 44), Nineveh (Jonah 3), Babylon (2 Kings 25:27–30; Psalm 137; Ezekiel; Daniel), Ecbatana (Ezra 6:2) and Susa (Nehemiah 1:1–2:8; Esther), not to mention all 127 provinces, from India to Ethiopia, of king Ahasuerus's empire (Esther 9:1–5).

The conventional claim that the Jewish diaspora existed in every nation of the known world, which was not far from the literal truth, is echoed in Luke's reference to 'Jews from every nation under heaven' in Jerusalem for the feast of Pentecost (Acts 2:5). The list that follows of fifteen peoples or places is a reasonably accurate account of the extent of the Jewish diaspora (2:9–11). Its outer limits are notably rather less extended than those of the Genesis 10 table of nations, except in the east, where Luke's list begins with the Parthians. But in the north it reaches only the southern shore of the Black Sea, in the south no further than Arabia (probably Nabatea in north-west Arabia), in the west Rome. None of these are even close to the ends of the earth according to the geography of the time, and Luke certainly knows this. He himself refers elsewhere to Ethiopia (Acts 8:27),[28] while the New Testament also knows of Spain (Romans 15:24) and the Scythians (Colossians 3:11), and everyone at this time knew of India and of the northern coast of Europe. But Luke's sketch of the Jewish diaspora is limited to places where there were significant Jewish communities, as well as probably the need to place Jerusalem centrally, which it does with considerable accuracy. This is the Jewish world to which the gospel was to go out from Jerusalem, thereby also reaching the Gentile nations among whom the Jews lived. It makes clear how the Christian mission took its form from the Israel-centred world of the Old Testament and, equally importantly, from the inseparability, both historical and

---

[28] Byron, *Symbolic Blackness and Ethnic Difference in Early Christian Literature*, p. 111, argues that 'those who are far away' in Acts 2:39 refers to the Ethiopians and anticipates the conversion of the Ethiopian in 8:26–39. 'Far away' can describe the nations at the ends of the earth in biblical (Isaiah 33:13; 49:12; 57:19; 66:19) and non-biblical usage. Luke probably does continue here the image of 'the end of the earth' that he evoked in Acts 1:8, and surely intends not only Ethiopia but all the ends of the earth. But it is true that the Ethiopian of Acts 8 is the only inhabitant of any of the ends of the earth who appears in his narrative.

eschatological, of Israel's destiny from that of the nations among whom Israel was placed by God and throughout whom Israel had been scattered by God.

3. Seeking and sending – or: from here to there, from there to here

Studies of the precedents for missionary thinking in the Old Testament and of the beginnings of missionary practice in the New Testament frequently contrast two directions of movement: the centripetal and the centrifugal.[29] ('Centripetal' refers to movement in towards a centre, 'centrifugal' to movement out from a centre. So the issue concerns the direction of movement in relation to Jerusalem, the centre: moving in to Jerusalem or out from Jerusalem?) The expectation in the Old Testament prophets that the nations will come to acknowledge and to serve the God of Israel is usually depicted as the coming of the nations to Jerusalem, to the centre where God is present and worshipped (e.g. Zechariah 8:20–23; 14:16) – a centripetal movement. It is this centripetal movement that is also envisaged in sayings of Jesus. When he foresees that many will come from the east and from the west and eat with the patriarchs in the kingdom of God (Matthew 8:11; cf. Luke 13:29),[30] Jesus seems most obviously to be echoing prophecies of the return of

---

[29] E.g. J. Blauw, *The Missionary Nature of the Church: A Survey of the Biblical Theology of Mission* (Guildford/London: Lutterworth, 1962); J. Jeremias, *Jesus' Promise to the Nations*, S. H. Hooke (tr.) (SBT 24; London: SCM Press, 1958).

[30] Luke's version refers to all four points of the compass. Both have precedent in the Old Testament prophecies: Zechariah 8:7 (east and west); Isaiah 11:12 (from the four corners of the earth); 43:5–6 (east, west, north, south, from far away, from the end of the earth); 49:12 (from far away, north, west, Syene [south]).

the Jewish diaspora to Jerusalem (e.g. Zechariah 8:7–8; Isaiah 11:12; Isaiah 43:5–6; 49:12; Psalm 107:3), but the prophets also pictured the Gentile nations coming with the returning Jewish exiles from all directions to Zion (Isaiah 49:22–23; 60:1–9; 66:20; Zechariah 8:23). Also implying the centripetal image is Jesus' saying about the community his disciples should compose: 'A city set on a hill cannot be hidden' (Matthew 5:14). It recalls the prophecy found in both Isaiah and Micah about mount Zion, standing as the highest of all mountains, so that all the nations stream to it (Isaiah 2:2; Micah 4:1). Jesus' disciples are to be a centre of attraction to which others will come.

By contrast with these centripetal images, the New Testament's understanding of mission is usually said to be novel, not in its expectation of the conversion of the Gentile nations, but in the idea of mission to them, i.e. of going out from the centre to the periphery, a centrifugal movement. In fact, there are already some hints of this in the prophets, most obviously, as we have noticed, in Isaiah 66:19. In the prophecy of Isaiah and Micah, just mentioned, not only do the nations come to Zion but the word of the LORD goes out from Zion (Isaiah 2:3; Micah 4:2). The image of Zion glowing with the light of God's glory, shining out into the darkness, such that the nations are drawn to Zion (Isaiah 60:1–3; cf. Matthew 5:14–15; Philippians 2:15), combines both movements: light goes out and draws the nations in. The idea of people taking the good news of salvation out from Zion to the nations is a variation on this image, not a completely different idea. When Jesus places side by side, as warning examples to his hearers, the prophet Jonah and the Queen of Sheba, he draws from Scripture both a centripetal image and a centrifugal image: Jonah is sent from Israel to Nineveh in the north, while the Queen of the South is drawn to Jerusalem from the ends of the earth by the reputation of Solomon's wisdom (Matthew 12:41–42). Mission is not the explicit point in this saying of Jesus, but these are two Old Testament foreshadowings, different and complementary, of the way people will come to know the good news about Jesus himself. The centrifugal and centripetal images are not mutually exclusive, and this is especially the case when, as we shall see, the geography becomes more metaphorical than literal.

The dominant centrifugal image in the Bible is that of the sending of an individual. This image is frequently used of God's sending a prophet to God's own people (Moses, Isaiah, Jeremiah, Ezekiel, Jesus himself), and in such cases there is little, if any, sense of geographical movement entailed. The image is rather of authorization to speak and to act in God's name, and this meaning is retained in the sending of disciples by God or Jesus (e.g. John 20:21; Romans 10:15; 1 Corinthians 1:17; cf. Matthew 28:18–20). Especially when used of sending to other nations, it acquires a more strongly geographical nuance, as already in Isaiah's prophecy of the survivors who will be sent to the nations (Isaiah 66:19) and then in the sending of apostles in Acts (Acts 13:4; 22:21; 26:17). 'Go, for I will send you *far away* to the Gentiles,' says Jesus to Paul in his vision in the Temple (Acts 22:21), evoking that familiar Isaianic image of the very distant nations (Isaiah 33:13; 49:12; 57:19; 66:19; cf. Daniel 9:7; Acts 2:39). But even in these cases authorization to speak remains a significant dimension of the meaning. There is a significant exception to the rule that the sending is usually of individuals: John's Gospel (despite what has sometimes been called its individualism)[31] seems to envisage a corporate sending by Jesus of the

---

[31] C. F. D. Moule, 'The Individualism of the Fourth Gospel', *Novum Testamentum* 5 (1962), pp. 171–90.

community of his disciples, especially when the sending (17:18) is closely connected with Jesus' prayer that his disciples should be one, as Jesus and the Father are one (17:20–23).[32]

The literal geographical use of these images depends on the idea of the centrality of Jerusalem, which the earliest Christian mission certainly assumed and to which the book of Acts continues to refer when Jesus tells the apostles they are to be his witnesses in Jerusalem, in Judea and Samaria, and to the ends of the earth (Acts 1:8). This Zion-centred geography is important even for the way Paul conceived his mission, describing it in Romans as following an arc with its centre in Jerusalem,[33] which he now wishes to complete by visiting Rome not primarily as a destination in itself but as a staging-post on the way to Spain, the western end of the earth (Romans 15:19, 23–24). Paul evidently conceived his collection for the Jerusalem church as some form of the pilgrimage of the nations to Jerusalem, bringing the tribute or the offering that so many of the prophecies mention. Yet, even though the Jerusalem church seems to have held axiomatically to the centrality of Jerusalem, that church itself already had the conceptual means of metaphorizing this geographical image and making Jerusalem itself dispensable for the Christian mission. The new temple, the temple of the messianic age, was, they believed, the church itself, not a building but the community (cf. Galatians 2:9). The community was the place of God's eschatological presence, and it was this notion of the new Temple as the Christian community that made it possible for the Jerusalem leaders to accept that Gentile converts could be

---

[32] A. J. Köstenberger, *The Missions of Jesus and the Disciples according to the Fourth Gospel* (Grand Rapids, Michigan: Eerdmans, 1998), pp. 188–90.

[33] See Scott, *Paul and the Nations*, pp. 136–40.

fully members of the messianic people of God without
having to become Jews. If the community were defined by
the Temple on mount Zion, this would not be possible,
since Gentiles were excluded. But the prophecies of the
nations seeking God's presence in the Temple could be
fulfilled in the community of Jews and Gentiles that God
himself was building as his new Temple. This is part of
James's decisive argument at the Jerusalem conference in
Acts 15,[34] and the image of the church as the new Temple
is found widely through the New Testament literature.

So with the idea of a new Temple that was not a location, but a people, we can see the spatial image of the
centre and the periphery beginning to lose its literal geographical reference. This happens very strikingly when
Ephesians speaks of 'those who were far off' and 'those
who were near', language borrowed from Isaiah 57:19
and used to refer to Gentile and Jewish members of
the church, respectively insiders and outsiders to God's
covenant with Israel, able and not able to enter God's
presence in the Temple (Ephesians 2:12). In the church
both have access to God in Christ. God's presence is now
among his people in the metaphorical Temple they themselves compose (2:21). This new centre is everywhere and
nowhere, just as with the advent of modern geography
and postmodern globalization the ends of the earth are
now everywhere and nowhere. To substitute another
physical centre for Jerusalem, whether Rome or Byzan-
tium in earlier times or western Europe in the modern age
of missions, was always a mistake, however understand-
able. God's people move from place to place, but not

---

[34] R. Bauckham, 'James and the Gentiles (Acts 15.13–21)' in B.
Witherington III (ed.), *History, Literature and Society in the
Book of Acts* (Cambridge: Cambridge University Press, 1996),
pp. 154–84; J. Ådna, 'James' Position at the Summit Meeting of
the Apostles and the Elders in Jerusalem (Acts 15)' in Ådna and
Kvalbein (eds), *The Mission of the Early Church*, pp. 87–123.

from a geographical centre to a geographical periphery. Mission, to borrow the title of Bishop Michael Nazir-Ali's book, is 'from everywhere to everywhere'.[35]

This Christian abandonment of the idea of a specific geographical centre should not be misunderstood along the lines of the idea, much too often encountered, that the Old Testament is particularistic and the New Testament universalistic. In both testaments there is continual movement from the particular to the universal. In biblical terms we cannot have the universal without the particular. That Christians no longer have a single geographical *centre* by no means abolishes this general principle. It simply means that one specific case of the movement from particular to the universal – movement from the single centre of the world to the periphery of the world – is no longer literally applicable.

The permanent value of the image of the two directions of movement – centrifugal and centripetal – is not tied to any particular geography, though it will always, like all human life, have geographical contexts. The church's mission requires both the individuals and groups who, authorized by God to communicate his message, go out from the community to others, near or far, and also the community that manifests God's presence in its midst by its life together and its relationships to others. The image of witness, not a geographical one but one which lies near the heart of the biblical understanding of mission, important in Isaiah, John, Acts and Revelation, transcends the two aspects. (We shall return to this missiological motif of witness in the last chapter.)

However, before leaving the Jerusalem-centred geographical images, we should notice that, while in some parts of the New Testament they are metaphorized in an

---

[35] M. Nazir-Ali, *From Everywhere to Everywhere* (London: Collins, 1991).

ecclesiological way, that is, in terms of the Christian community, in the Fourth Gospel they are metaphorized in a christological way, that is, with reference to Jesus. In John Jesus himself is the new Temple who transcends the sacred locatedness of God's presence on mount Zion. Thus, speaking to the Samaritan woman, Jesus not only affirms rather bluntly the Jewish position in the Jewish–Samaritan debate about the true place of God's presence in the land of Israel (4:22), but also declares this geographical issue superseded, for 'the hour is coming when you will worship the Father neither on this mountain [Mount Gerizim] nor in Jerusalem' (4:21, cf. 23). At a stroke Jesus here metaphorizes all the prophecies of the centrality of Zion in the messianic age. All, as we know more clearly from other passages in the Fourth Gospel, are fulfilled in Jesus himself as the one in whom God is to be encountered and known. Similarly also, Jesus himself is the light of the world that shines in the darkness so that those who will may come to the light (1:9; 8:12; 12:46).

The most interesting use of the centripetal image in John is this saying of Jesus: 'I, when I am lifted up from the earth, will draw all people to myself' (12:32). There may well be a background in Isaiah 11:10, 12, where the Davidic Messiah is described as the signal that God will raise up as a rallying point for the nations from the four corners of the earth. In John the ensign for the nations becomes Jesus lifted up high above the earth on the cross – and, thereby, also exalted to heaven. It is the crucified and exalted Jesus who draws all people to himself, like the exalted mount Zion to which, in the prophecies, all the nations stream.

Two points about this rich image are worth noticing. One is that what happens here is what happens in the church's mission, but Jesus himself, the crucified and exalted one, is the agent. It is he who draws all people to himself. David Bosch observes that, in the Old Testament, the centripetal movement is not, as such, the dominant characteristic of 'mission',[36] but is 'employed to give expression to the conviction that God, not Israel, is the author of mission'.[37] Similarly, in this saying of Jesus in John, the centripetal image makes clear that it is Jesus who draws people to himself, a point which is not so clear in the centrifugal image of the disciples sent out by Jesus to continue his mission, also an important image in John (20:21).

Secondly, while in a sense geography is transcended in this image – people are not drawn to a specific place – particularity most emphatically remains. It is the particular human person Jesus, crucified and exalted, who draws all people and to whom all people are drawn. As always in Scripture, universality is not despite but by way of particularity. Jesus, the Messiah for all people, the Saviour for all people, has all the temporal and geographical particularity of a genuinely human person. He lived in Galilee and Judea in the first century. As the crucified and exalted one all the particularity of his earthly life and fate, as the gospels tell it, still belongs to his identity, while his exaltation enables him to relate, in that particularity, to all human beings as he could not have done during his earthly life itself. This saying in John is in fact Jesus' eventual response to the Greeks who approached the disciples wishing to see Jesus (12:20–21). For members of the nations to see him at that point, before his death, was of no consequence, since he is about to be lifted up above the earth where all will be able to see

---

[36] The word is not strictly appropriate with reference to the centripetal image, but I use it here because Bosch does.

[37] D. J. Bosch, *Witness to the World: The Christian Mission in Theological Perspective* (London: Marshall, Morgan & Scott, 1980), p. 77.

him and to come to him. Finally, Jesus does not so much replace the Jewish particularity of the Temple on mount Zion as fulfil it. Its particularity becomes part of his, since his own human particularity was and is Jewish, that of a Jewish man who himself worshipped in what he called his Father's house (Luke 2:49; John 2:16).

4. A diaspora people

As well as the two geographical images, the centripetal and the centrifugal, that we have discussed so far, there is also a third geographical image, which comes into its own with the loss or the lack of a physical centre. This is the image of God's people as exiles among the nations. The image, of course, originated in Old Testament Israel's experience of deportation and exile. Luke's account of the movement of the gospel from Jerusalem outwards depicts a literal diaspora of the Jerusalem church, driven by persecution from Jerusalem, some as far as Antioch, where the Gentile mission first began in earnest. With the loss of a sense of a physical centre of the Christian movement in Jerusalem, the way is clear for writers like the authors of Hebrews and 1 Peter to represent Christians anywhere as aliens and exiles among the nations, sojourning like the patriarchs in lands that are not their own, awaiting their homecoming to the heavenly Jerusalem that will come down to earth in the future.[38] In modern times this image has sometimes suffered from association with a non-biblical kind of otherworldliness, but its positive significance for mission is its call to the church to be a counter-cultural movement, living for a different God in a different way and with a different future in view.

---

[38] Hebrews 11:8–16; 13:14; 1 Peter 1:1; 2:11–12; 5:13.

It may be that this image will come into its own again as the church in the postmodern west reconceptualizes its missionary relationship to a post-Christian society. The church in the west may have to get used to the idea that its own centre in God, from which it goes out to others in proclamation and compassion, is actually a position of social and cultural exile or marginality. This may improve its witness to the Christ who was himself so often found at the margins.

Chapter 4

Witness to the Truth in a Postmodern and Globalized World

1. The biblical story and the postmodern critique

Lesslie Newbigin published a fine book on Christian mission, *The Open Secret*, subtitled *Sketches for a Missionary Theology*, in 1978. In it he has a chapter entitled 'The Gospel in World History', which summarizes much that I have tried to say in the earlier chapters of this book in a different way, with more attention to detailed exegesis. He too poses as 'the center of the question of missions' the problem of universality and particularity in the biblical narrative:

> [I]t is the problem of relating God's universality to his particular deeds and words. God is over all and in all, and not a sparrow falls to the ground without his will. Yet the Bible talks of God acting and speaking in particular times and places. How are these related?

As a valuable illustration of how this issue implicates the church's mission he refers to Romans 10:12–15, where Paul, as he says, 'makes a statement of sweeping universality':

there is no distinction between Jew and Greek; the same
Lord is Lord of all and is generous to all who call on him.
For [Paul quotes the prophet Joel], 'Everyone who calls on
the name of the Lord shall be saved.'

(Romans 10:12–13 NRSV)

But this assertion of universality leads Paul immediately
and necessarily, by the logic of his understanding of
the biblical narrative, to 'the assertion of the need for the
missionary to go and preach':[1]

But how are they to call on one in whom they have not
believed? And how are they to believe in one of whom they
have never heard? And how are they to hear without some-
one to proclaim him? And how are they to proclaim him
unless they are sent?

(Romans 10:14–15a, NRSV)

Mission takes place between the highly particular history
of Jesus and the universal goal of God's coming kingdom.

To understand the Bible's way of relating the particular
and the universal, Newbigin expounds a biblical understanding of election. This is in effect what I have also done
without using that term (since it raises other theological
expectations I did not want to be distracted by). In
Chapter 2 I spoke of how God *singles out* individuals and
groups to be the bearers of God's blessing for all. God's
purpose never ends with the particular but moves on
from particular to particular in the direction of the
universal. Newbigin helpfully relates this pattern of
the divine purpose to something very fundamental about
human nature as the Bible and the Christian tradition
understand it:

---

[1] L. Newbigin, *The Open Secret: Sketches for a Missionary Theology*
(London/Grand Rapids, Michigan: SPCK/Eerdmans, 1978), p. 74.

If each human being is be ultimately understood as an independent spiritual monad, then salvation could only be through an action directed impartially to each and all.[2] But if the truly human is the shared reality of mutual and collective responsibility which the Bible envisages, then salvation must be an action which binds us together and restores for us the true mutual relation to each other and the true shared relation to the world of nature. This would mean that the gift of salvation would be bound up with our openness to one another. It would have to pass from one to the other. It would not come to each, direct from above, like a shaft of light through the roof. It would come from the neighbor in the action by which we open the door to invite the neighbor in. But the neighbor would have to be sent (Rom 10:14). There would have to be one called and chosen to be the bearer of the blessing. The blessing is intended for all. But the blessing itself would be negated if it were not given and received in a way that binds each to other. God's way of universal salvation, if it is to be addressed to man [*sic*] as he really is and not to the abstraction of a detached 'soul,' must be accomplished by the way of election – of choosing, calling, and sending one to be the bearer of blessing for all.[3]

This is important. I should want to add that the movement from the particular to the universal is required not only by the interconnectedness of human life in the world, but also by the way that this God is known. We know God most adequately when the universal God particularizes himself, identifies himself for us as the God of Abraham, Isaac and Jacob, and as the God of

---

[2] It is worth noticing how this, the more typically eastern religious approach, correlates, even if only superficially, with the excessive individualism of contemporary western society. This accounts for the popularity of eastern religions and spiritualities of a similar type in the west.

[3] Newbigin, *The Open Secret*, pp. 78–9.

Jesus Christ. God's concrete history with Israel and in
Jesus is who God is for us. In this particularity God is
different and can be known.

In his chapter Newbigin faced a difficulty in the
modern world for the Bible's claim to be, as he puts it, 'a
universal history'.[4] How can this be related to the story of
humanity as it is told in a modern history of the world?
His answer is that all interpretation of history arises not
merely from the historical data but also from the presup-
positions, axioms, models and paradigms we bring to the
data. The Christian relates to a story, the biblical story,
that is part of the whole fabric of human history, but
which the Bible claims and the Christian believes dis-
closes the meaning of the whole of history.[5] Essential to
this disclosure is the claim that, whereas the point of a
story only becomes clear at its end, the biblical story
reveals the point of the whole human story even before its
end has been reached.[6] Newbigin concludes: 'Christian
faith is thus a way of understanding world history which
challenges and relativizes all other models by which the
meaning of history is interpreted.'[7] Among other models
he seems especially to have in mind the Enlightenment
idea of human progress.[8]

At the time when Newbigin wrote he was able to
assume that writing a universal history and seeking an
overall meaning in the whole of history would be an
acceptable enterprise, at least for western readers. (He
considers that 'the idea of universal history', not to be
found in the great religions of Asia, 'has come into our

---

[4] Ibid., p. 91.
[5] Ibid., pp. 98–9. Here, and at other points in this discussion,
   Newbigin's thought seems inspired by the work of Wolfhart
   Pannenberg, though he does not refer to him.
[6] Ibid., p. 95.
[7] Ibid., p. 99.
[8] Ibid., pp. 9–7.

culture from the Bible'.)[9] But this was soon to be influentially challenged. Only a year after the publication of Newbigin's book the French philosopher Jean-François Lyotard published a definition of the postmodern that has become famous in relevant circles.[10] He defined the postmodern as incredulity towards grand narratives or metanarratives. Under Lyotard's influence many thoughtful people in the west have come to see metanarratives as characteristic of modernity, disbelief in metanarratives and opposition to metanarratives as characteristic of postmodernity.

These are terms I introduced briefly in Chapter 1. A metanarrative is an attempt to tell a single story about the whole of human history in order to attribute a single and integrated meaning to the whole. People who advance such a grand narrative are claiming to be able to interpret, to bring within a single interpretative framework, all the diversity of human history, life and culture. Some people call this a 'totalizing' framework – one which tries to subsume everything within its concept of the truth. In the opening section of Chapter 1 I quoted Chief Rabbi Jonathan Sacks' reference to universalist cultures which claim to possess a universal truth that must be valid for everyone. Such cultures tell a metanarrative, a grand story about all of history and its meaning. One such culture was the modern western culture stemming from the Enlightenment of the eighteenth century: its metanarrative was the idea of progress. Humanity is supposed to be on a path of progress towards a better, ultimately Utopian, future. The rationalist values of western modernity were taken to be universal values, so that their

---

[9] Ibid., p. 96.
[10] J.-F. Lyotard, *The Postmodern Condition*, G. Bennington and B. Massumi (trs) (Minneapolis: University of Minnesota Press, 1984), p. xxiv.

propagation was the natural good of all, and the super-session of all local cultures by the self-evident goods of western modernity was progress. The means of progress were education, technology and imperialism.

Lesslie Newbigin, writing in 1978, could assume that, in a western context, the argument was between different metanarratives. The Christian metanarrative, the story the Bible tells, with (among other characteristics) its special understanding of the relationship between the particular and the universal, could be seen as an alternative to various secular narratives, such as the idea of progress and Marxism. What arrived with Jean-François Lyotard's definition of the postmodern as incredulity towards metanarratives was a radical critique of meta-narratives as such.

Postmodernism, as defined by Lyotard and others, is rejection of all metanarratives, because, as attempts to universalize one's own values or culture, they are neces-sarily authoritarian or oppressive. They can subsume difference only by suppressing it. Postmodernism exposes metanarratives as projects of power and domination. In place of such universal pretensions postmodernism opts for particularity, diversity, localism, relativism. Post-modernism is not only the inability to believe in any metanarrative; it is a principled espousal of diversity and heterogeneity against universalism and unity. While post-modernism is explicitly opposed to the metanarratives of western modernity, it is implicitly critical also of older metanarratives, such as those of Christianity and Islam. From this perspective of such suspicion towards all meta-narratives, much that Newbigin said in his book and much that I have said in this book would seem highly suspicious.

This then is where we resume our discussion (broached in Chapter 1) with Jonathan Sacks' (rather postmodern

Jewish, as I called it in Chapter 1) critique of the cultural imperialism of the great universalist cultures. In that initial engagement with Sacks I questioned his way of relating the particular and the universal, and in what I have said subsequently I have been expounding the biblical story as a narrative movement from particularity to universality. By now addressing the critique that this would seem to invite from a postmodern critic we shall be able to understand more fully some special characteristics of the biblical metanarrative which distinguish it crucially from the metanarratives of modernity.

So let us frame the criticism we need to address. Is not the narrative movement of the Bible from particularity to universality, which has been the main theme of this book, a kind of narrative imperialism or ecclesiastical globalization, a form of self-aggrandizement on the church's part, by which the church universalizes its own story, foists it on others, subjects others to it, suppresses their own stories and deprives them of the opportunity to write their own stories? Is it not even the case, it might be asked, that the Christian church's drive to universalize its own story at others' expense is the root of the whole modern phenomenon of totalizing narratives from the Enlightenment idea of progress, through European imperialism, Marxism, Nazism, down to global capitalism and the Americanization of the world, with all the implications for violent suppression and ideological repression of human freedom and diversity? That some of these narratives have indeed applied a veneer of Christianity to justify themselves and that the church and its mission have sometimes been implicated in both the brighter and the darker sides of these manifestations of modernity cannot be denied. Our question must be whether the *biblical narrative* of movement from the particular to the universal has anything which essentially distinguishes it from such dubious totalization. Or must we take refuge in a radical pluralism which can tolerate only local narratives with no pretensions to wider relevance and renounce altogether the desire for meaning that requires some kind of sketch of the meaning of the whole if we are to live meaningful stories of our own? At stake is not only the human quest for narrative meaning but also the claims of a God who is not radically unknowable.

2. The biblical story as a non-modern metanarrative

When Lyotard rejected grand narratives he was not thinking of the Christian story. A metanarrative as he defined it is a characteristically modern, post-Enlightenment phenomenon. This does not make his critique entirely irrelevant to the biblical metanarrative, but it does require us to be careful to distinguish this from the secular metanarratives of the modern period. Lyotard's direct targets are the various forms of the project of modern reason that aspires to a comprehensive explanation of reality, including the human condition, and seeks thereby rationally based universal criteria by which to order society and to liberate humanity through technology. A modern metanarrative is a totalizing theory which aims to subsume all events, all perspectives and all forms of knowledge in a comprehensive rational explanation. It presumes that reality, both nature and human history, is fundamentally comprehensible to reason, and can therefore be subjected to rational mastery in the interests of human progress. In the postmodern critique, such a metanarrative is an ideological tool of western domination of the world.

In Chapter 1 I warned against the temptation to assimilate the biblical story to the modern idea of progress. The coming of the kingdom of God is not a matter of cumulative progress over time. Moreover, the biblical story is decidedly not one of human mastery. It does not, like the modern myth of progress, describe the human achievement of human goals or even a process of immanent reason at work in the historical process. It views history in terms of the freedom and purpose of God and of human freedom to obey or to resist God. History is not open to rational comprehension and mastery, but becomes comprehensible only in so far as God reveals his purposes and fulfils them. Human agency in history is, of course, important and is celebrated in the Bible where appropriate, but its success follows divine initiative and requires divine concurrence. Its results are not susceptible to more than limited calculation. There is ample room for contingency in history, in the sense that much, perhaps most, of what occurs is not the result of intended human action. The biblical story certainly does, in an important sense, disclose the meaning of the whole, but not in such a way as to make history transparent to its divinely intended purpose. In much that happens, God's purpose remains inscrutable, as Paul observed, following his most adventurous attempt to discern God's purpose in Paul's own Gentile mission: 'How unsearchable are his judgments and how inscrutable his ways!' (Romans 11:33).

It is important that our thinking about mission takes seriously these differences from the typically modern view of history as a human project to be achieved by human mastery. As I pointed out in Chapter 1, mission is God's work before and after it is ours. The results of our witness are not calculable. Mission must certainly be contextualized, but it must also be open to the possibilities the biblical narrative opens up for us as what is possible in God's gift. God continually makes more of what we do for him than we can make of it ourselves, and God continually prevents the harm our foolishness and failures would do. The Bible does not map out for us the path from Pentecost to the kingdom. It invites our trust in God rather than mastery or calculation of history. God can be trusted to be faithful to his promises, but he remains free in his fulfilment of them. As we should certainly have learned from the biblical story, there will be both shocks and surprises. God's action is disruptive at least as often as it is continuous with what might have been expected. In many ways, therefore, mission is not the imposing of predetermined patterns on to history, but openness to the incalculable ways of God in history.

Also relevant here is the considerable extent to which the Bible does *not* have a carefully plotted single story-line, like, for example, a conventional novel. It is a sprawling collection of narratives along with much non-narrative material that stands in a variety of relationships to the narratives. Major stretches of the main narrative are told more than once in significantly divergent ways (consider, for example, the four gospels or, in the Old Testament, the books of Kings and Chronicles). This plurality of angles on the same subject matter disrupts any expectations of a single perspective for the reader to adopt unproblematically. Rather we are encouraged to view the same events from varying perspectives. Then there is the profusion and sheer untidiness of the narrative materials: the proliferation of little stories within the larger ones, the narrative directions left unfinished, the narrative hints that enlist readers' imagination, the ambiguity of stories that leave their meanings open, the narrative fragments of the stories of prophets or apostles in their books, the references to stories external to Scripture, as well as non-narrative materials that challenge the adequacy of the narratives. All this makes any sort of *finality* in summarizing the biblical story inconceivable. The Bible itself offers no summary of the whole story from beginning to end. It contains a number of summaries of parts of the narrative, but again their divergence is often as great as their coincidence. Summaries of the biblical story are more or less essential, but they cannot replace what they summarize, and the latter, as they say, resists closure. In other words, the biblical story refuses to be summed up in a finally adequate interpretation that would never need to be revised or replaced. As this book has illustrated, plotting the lines of narrative development in the Bible as a whole is always a task at which readers have to *work*.

Those who try to map the broad outlines of the biblical narrative, discerning the purposes of God portrayed in it, are often tempted to override the untidy complexity of the actual narrative and non-narrative contents of Scripture. For the systematic theological mind the little stories too awkwardly resist their easy assimilation into an overall plot. There are too many fragments that seem to lead nowhere and too many that seem to point in opposite directions. It is tempting to take the principle of a canonical hermeneutic, that the parts must be understood in the light of the whole, as a reason for simply suppressing the not readily assimilable parts. But these inescapable features of the actual narrative form of Scripture surely have a message in themselves: that the particular has its own integrity that should not be suppressed for the sake of a too readily comprehensible universal. The Bible does, in some sense, tell an overall story that encompasses all its other contents, but this story is not a sort of straitjacket that reduces all else to a narrowly defined uniformity. It is a story that is hospitable to considerable diversity and to tensions, challenges and even seeming contradictions of its own claims.

3. The biblical story and economic globalization

One response to the postmodern rejection of all metanarratives is to point out that, like it or not, we live in a global world and to do so responsibly we surely need to think globally.[11] Globalization, according to Anthony Giddens, Director of the London School of Economics, 'is the way we now live'.[12] The reality of our world is not the end of grand narratives, but the increasing dominance of the narrative of economic globalization. Here again we return to a notion I introduced Chapter 1. By economic globalization I refer to the global spread of free-market economics and the culture it entails, consumerist individualism, all dominated by the multinational corporations with their bases in the United States and other western countries. This is the new imperialism, an economic as distinct from the political and economic imperialism of the past, and representing, in fact, the domination of politics by capitalist economics. Globalization as an ideology has grown out of the older idea of progress but differs in that it reduces progress to economic growth, which is supposed to bring all other goods in its train. We can quite appropriately call it a metanarrative because it entails a worldview, a notion of the human good (the American consumerist dream of wealth and glamour), and because it tells a story in which the universal dominance of unfettered capitalism is both

---

[11] T. Eagleton, *The Illusions of Postmodernism* (Oxford: Blackwell, 1996).

[12] A. Giddens, *Runaway World: How Globalization is Reshaping our Lives* (London: Profile, 1999), p. 19.

irresistible and beneficent. It is also readily susceptible to the postmodern critique of metanarratives as ways of legitimating oppression. There is no doubt that globalization has made the rich countries richer and the poor poorer (while also widening the gap between rich and poor within each country). Its ideology, while purporting to benefit all, serves the interests of the rich and powerful. This is surely inevitable with an economic system oriented to the maximization of profit and the accumulation of wealth rather than to the meeting of basic human needs.

To substantiate the point that the gap between rich and poor countries has widened as a result of globalization, the following figures speak for themselves.[13]

3.1 Share of global income over time

Year	Richest 20%	Poorest 20%	Ratio of Rich/Poor
1960	70.2	2.3	30:1
1970	73.9	2.3	32:1
1980	76.3	1.7	45:1
1989	82.7	1.4	59:1
1997	90.0	1.0	74:1

Christians must not be seduced by the enticing notion that economic growth as such is self-evidently a prime good for humanity. We must probe the facts behind this glib assumption and ask questions about who and what is benefited or damaged by the actual economic growth

---

[13] W. Ellwood, *The No-Nonsense Guide to Globalization* (London: Verso, 2001), p. 101.

that we are considering. About economic growth we should be asking at least three very testing questions: (a) Does it benefit the poorest people? (b) Does it destroy the environment? (c) Does it destroy other (traditional) values which are at least as important as economic prosperity? Not only on the first but also on the other two counts economic globalization as it has recently occurred and is currently occurring is surely blatantly guilty of impoverishing and vandalizing God's world.

It is interesting how analyses of the world system of economic globalization show that world-pictures which have a centre and a periphery may not after all be so outdated. Morris Berman, for example, speaks of a so-called core of privileged countries and a periphery of exploited countries:

> Core countries are those in the privileged regions of the Northern Hemisphere such as the United States and Western Europe. It is in these regions that financial, technical, and productive (usually industrial) power is concentrated, power that is controlled by an elite. The periphery, on the other hand, contains the exploited regions that sell their resources and labor to the core without ever having access to the latter's wealth. The enrichment of the core is structurally dependent on the impoverishment of the periphery.[14]

This kind of globalization is the new imperialism.[15] It continues the kind of oppression that modern meta-narratives of progress have always legitimated, but now implemented by the modern media and modern information technology. It has to be said that the western

---

[14] M. Berman, *The Twilight of American Culture* (London: Duckworth, 2001), p. 39.

[15] Cf. R. Biel, *The New Imperialism: Crisis and contradictions in North-South relations* (London/New York: Zed, 2000).

postmodern critique offers no cogent or effective resistance to it. Its relativism is too easily assimilated to economic pragmatism. (As Peter Selby comments, 'Relativism is frankly more profitable.')[16] What do we really need in order to recognize and to resist this new metanarrative of globalization? Surely a story that counters the global dominance of the profit-motive and the culture of consumption with a powerful affirmation of universal values? But the Christian metanarrative can adopt this role only if it resists becoming a tool of the forces of domination.

Can Christianity sufficiently detach itself from its own undoubted collusions with the oppressive metanarratives of western imperialism and progress to remain, between modern grand narrative and postmodern relativism, something else? One would think it should be easier for the church to distinguish itself from the forces of economic globalization than it used to be for the church to distinguish itself from western colonialism and cultural imperialism. After all, in the nineteenth and early twentieth centuries western culture really was more Christian than it is now, and so it was all too easy to confuse witness to Jesus with exporting western 'Christian' culture. Now that western culture is increasingly post- and even anti-Christian, the distinction should be easier to make and to show.

It may well be that, only if Christianity in the west becomes a movement of resistance to such evils as consumerism, excessive individualism and the exploitation of the global periphery, can Christianity in many other parts of the world be credibly distinguished from

---

[16] P. Selby, 'The Silent Word Still Speaks: Globalization and the Interpretation of Scripture' in C. Reed (ed.), *Development Matters: Christian Perspectives on Globalization* (London: Church House, 2001), p. 103.

the west's economic and cultural oppression of other cultures and peoples. Recall what I said in Chapter 2 about the biblical narrative as a movement that reaches all only by way of the least. Without international solidarity with the poorest of the world's poor the church's mission in any part of our globalized world is not only compromised but simply invalidated. It has departed from the biblical contours of God's way with the world.

Argentinian evangelical theologian René Padilla has called economic globalization 'the greatest challenge that the Christian mission faces' at the beginning of the twenty-first century.[17]

4. The biblical story and witness to truth

We must now return to the postmodern critique of metanarratives and our attempt to differentiate the biblical (non-modern) metanarrative from the modern metanarratives of mastery against which the postmodern critique is primarily directed. So far I have done this by highlighting the way the biblical story is open to God and not susceptible to rational calculation. But the postmodern critique also requires that we consider rather carefully the Christian claim to the *truth* of the biblical metanarrative.

For postmodernism any claim to universal truth is oppressive because it delegitimizes difference. I believe that in the end Christians must simply contest this preference for diversity over truth. It is not the case that diversity as such, any kind of diversity whatsoever, is a good in itself. It is not better for there to be people whose lives are blighted by destructive illusions than for their illusions to

---

[17] C. R. Padilla, 'Mission at the Turn of the Century/Millennium', *Evangel* 19/1 (2001), p. 6.

be dispelled. What is important is, firstly, that claims to universal truth should not be advanced as settled and closed. In the continuing openness of history, short of eschatological finality, claims to truth cannot but remain debatable. In fact, it is not the relativists, who care nothing for truth, but those who recognize and claim truth who can be genuinely open to dialogue and the truth of the other. But this also means, secondly, that assent to any claims to truth may not be coerced. Coercion contradicts the nature of truth. It opens the door to the distortion of truth into a vehicle of the will to power. There certainly are few more oppressive regimes than those that believe they stand for a truth that must be enforced. Because Christians have, sadly, in the past themselves treated Christianity as a truth to be enforced, we need to be very clear and resolute about this. It is in the very nature of Christian truth that it cannot be enforced. Coerce belief and you destroy belief and turn the truth believed into a lie.

Truth must be claimed in a way appropriate to the content of the truth. Scientific truth, for example, has its own means of claim and methods of verification. The image the Bible itself often suggests for the way its truth is to be claimed is that of witness. This is an extremely valuable image with which to meet the postmodern suspicion of all metanarratives as oppressive. Witness is non-coercive. It has no power but the convincingness of the truth to which it witnesses. Witnesses are not expected, like lawyers, to persuade by the rhetorical power of their speeches, but simply to testify to the truth for which they are qualified to give evidence. But to be adequate witness to the truth of God and the world, witness must be a lived witness involving the whole of life and even death. And as such it can show itself to be not self-serving. In our time witness is likely to be the main contender for truth against the various manifestations of the will to power.

Of course, we cannot consider the appropriateness of witness apart from the kind of truth to which it witnesses. The biblical motif of witness, drawn like so much of the New Testament's missionary conceptuality and vocabulary from the later chapters of Isaiah and developed especially in the Gospel of John and the book of Revelation, imagines history as a global contest for the truth in which the God of Israel and Jesus will demonstrate his true and sole deity to the nations. God's people are the witnesses to his truth and his great acts of salvation. The emphasis in this image is not so much on the authorization of a spokesperson, as in the image of a person sent or commissioned by God, but rather on the ability to speak from observation and experience of the God whose identity is not universally evident in the mere nature of things but must be known from his particular history with Israel and Jesus. He is indeed the Creator and Lord of all things, never more emphatically so than in the calls for all to acknowledge his true deity in Isaiah and Revelation, but who this Creator and Lord truly is appears from his particular history with Israel and Jesus. This is why the Scriptures often associate mission with the making known of God's name, as in the command to baptize in Matthew's great commission (Matthew 28:19). God's name names the narrative identity God gives himself in the biblical story. Witnesses, then, mediate the particularity of the biblical story and the universality of its claim.

Witness to this God is always also witness against idolatry, contending with the false witnesses to the idols who are no-gods.[18] The projects of the idols are indeed often projections of the aspirations and frustrations of

---

[18] Cf. V. Ramachandra, *Gods that Fail: Modern Idolatry and the Christian Mission* (Carlisle: Paternoster, 1996).

the human will to power. We should certainly think today, among others, of the greedy, never-satisfied idols that lurk behind the ideology of consumerism in its project to dominate the whole of life and the whole globe. To the domination of the no-gods, the rule of the true God is opposed not as a rival of the same kind but as qualitatively different. It must be characterized by telling the stories of the exodus from Pharaoh's tyranny, of the forms of human living together that are nourished by the Sinai covenant, of the suffering servant, of Jesus' proclamation and enactment of the kingdom, of his rejection and cross, of the discipleship and martyrdom of his followers. To put the same point differently, when Christians find their metanarrative in confrontation with an alternative, aggressive metanarrative – whether that of globalization or Islam or something else – nothing is more important than telling the biblical stories, especially that of Jesus, again and again. This is both an essential part of our witness and the way we retain our knowledge of what it is to which we witness. Without this witness to the qualitative difference of this God's rule, the Christian metanarrative like many others all too easily becomes an expression of the human will to power, as we can see from the more regrettable parts of Christian history.

For resisting the subversion of mission by the human will to power the first four chapters of 1 Corinthians are seminal. We already drew on them in Chapter 2. What Paul encounters there is not some Gnostic spiritualizing of the gospel message, as biblical scholars used to think, but a desire that the gospel message serve the projects of self-promotion and self-advancement that formed the social dynamic of Corinthian society. Paul confronts such projects with the cross of Christ that shows the gospel to be radically unassimilable to such projects.

When he states that in his preaching at Corinth he
decided to know nothing but Christ crucified (2:2),
he does not mean that he said nothing about God except
the cross. He means that he spoke of that God whose
narrative identity inescapably includes the cross. It is
significant (as we noticed in Chapter 2) that Paul's
account in fact appeals not only to the cross but also
extensively to the Old Testament characterization of
God as the one who characteristically chooses the powerless and the insignificant (1 Corinthians 1:19–21, 27–31;
3:18–20). In the cross God acts in character, in so far as
he is known from the biblical story, but also in a way that
is decisive for the plot of the biblical narrative's movement from the particular to the universal. Here, in the
crucified Christ, is God's self-identification as one human
being identified with all human beings, the particular
which is also the universally salvific, and that self-
identification is not with humanity in its self-aggrandizement, but with humanity in its degradation, humanity
victimized by the human will to power. All attempts to
co-opt this message to the projects of the will to power, to
make it an instrument of oppression, can do so only by
hiding the cross itself in the persuasive rhetoric Paul
renounced lest it deprive the cross of its power. Indeed, it
may be the power of the cross that can most effectively
break through the corrosive cynicism of much contemporary western culture, the suspicion that the will to power
is the hidden agenda in all human relationships however
apparently altruistic.[19]

Paul's account of the cross as the critical test of the
content of the church's witness is also – the themes are
intertwined in these early chapters of 1 Corinthians – an

---

[19] Cf. A. C. Thiselton, *Interpreting God and the Postmodern Self*
(Edinburgh: T&T Clark, 1995), pp. 159–63; Tomlin, *The
Power of the Cross*, pp. 297–307.

account of the cross as the critical test of the *form* of the church's witness. The way that, as an apostle of Christ, Paul lived and preached could serve the gospel only by not conforming to the social values and strategies that the message of the cross contradicts but the Corinthian Christians still espoused. That the church's mission is inseparable from the church's community life as the living of an alternative way in contradistinction to its sociocultural context is not always noticed to be as important in Paul as it is in the Sermon on the Mount or in James, but I think that in 1 Corinthians at least it is. But whereas God has, so to speak, plotted his own narrative identity irrevocably in the cross of Christ, the church's narrative identity in its mission remains unstable, in so far as its conformity to the cross is in question at every new juncture of its story and its faithfulness to the crucified God has to be sought and received in the face of ever-new temptations to self-aggrandizement.

5. Witness in the face of globalizing power

Can the biblical narrative resist, in a way that is true to the character of the biblical God's rule, the narratives of global power that dominate our world today? One element in an answer to this is the fact that the biblical metanarrative itself took shape partly in opposition to the globalizing powers of its day. Within the Bible, the biblical metanarrative is rarely portrayed as the dominant metanarrative in its world. Much more often it is up against the dominant narratives of the great empires from Pharaoh to Rome, all of whom told grand narratives of their divine right to rule. Characteristically they proclaimed their eternity (Isaiah 47:8; Revelation 18:7) and celebrated their divine achievement of universal rule

(Isaiah 14:13–14; Daniel 4:30; Revelation 13:5–8).
Theirs were certainly narratives of closure, justifying
oppression and suppressing dissent. It is against these
dominant narratives that the biblical metanarrative takes
on its most imperial and militant colours, especially in
the visions of Daniel and Revelation, which assert the
transcendent power of God over all would-be divine
rulers on earth and foresee their destruction and
supersession by the rule of God triumphant over all evil.
These visions construct a counter-narrative disputing
the imperial one, opening up a different way of seeing the
world. They empower non-violent resistance to oppression, enabling God's people to continue to refute the
finality and divinity of the empires. But they do not
suggest that the kingdom of God is merely a more powerful or more successful version of the imperial powers.
Their witness is to an altogether different kind of rule.[20]

To take a closer look at this we can resume our interest
in biblical geography. Luke's narrative of the birth of
Jesus begins with the information that 'a decree went out
from the Emperor Augustus that all the world should be
registered', i.e. for purposes of taxation (Luke 2:1). How
could the emperor Augustus decree that 'all the world'
should be registered? The word Luke uses (οἰκουμένη) is
the one that had been used from the time of Herodotus,

---

[20] E. S. Gerstenberger, '"World Dominion" in Yahweh Kingship
Psalms: Down to the Roots of Globalizing Concepts and
Strategies', *Horizons in Biblical Theology* 23 (2001), pp.
192–210, argues for a more positive, rather than polemical,
relationship between the ancient world empires and Israelite
ideas of the world dominion of YHWH, especially in the case of
the Persian Empire. In this latter case there is plausibility in this
approach. But it is notable that Gerstenberger does not discuss
the Babylonian or hellenistic empires, or the prophets or
Daniel, but focuses his argument on the psalms that portray
YHWH's universal rule non-polemically.

by Greek geographers, historians and others to refer to the whole inhabited world, the three continents of Europe, Asia and Africa, enclosed, as they believed, by the surrounding ocean. The Roman Empire did not extend to the boundaries of this world. To the east, for example, lay the extensive Parthian Empire, stretching from the Euphrates (though wars with Rome shifted the boundary from time to time) to the borders of India, and beyond the Parthian Empire lay India, whose extent would have been vague but certainly not negligible in the minds of inhabitants of the Roman Empire. Luke's statement is a gross exaggeration, but he merely – and deliberately – echoes the official ideology of the empire.

Rome inherited a project of world domination from the great empires of the east, whose similarly hyperbolic claims feature in the book of Daniel (Daniel 3:4, 7; 4:1; 5:19; 6:25; cf. Jeremiah 27:7). Conquest of the whole world was the declared aim of the Roman Empire and Augustus in particular claimed to have completed it.[21] In the *Res Gestae*, the record of his reign that Augustus left for posterity, he detailed his conquest of the whole inhabited world (*orbis terrarum*, the Latin equivalent of οἰκουμένη.[22] He recounted the long list of peoples who had been subjected to Rome during his reign, but special importance attached to the extension of Rome's power to the ends of the earth. This could not properly be described as conquest, but evidence of Rome's penetra-

---

[21] He was not the first; e.g. Pompey claimed to have 'extended the frontiers of the empire to the limits of the earth'. This claim was accompanied by a lengthy list of the kingdoms and territories he had conquered (C. Nicolet, *Space, Geography, and Politics in the Early Roman Empire* [Ann Arbor, Michigan: University of Michigan Press, 1991], p. 32).

[22] Ibid., ch. 1; J. M. Scott, *Geography in Early Judaism and Christianity* (SNTSMS 113; Cambridge: Cambridge University Press, 2002), ch. 1.

tion in some way to the most distant of lands was taken to indicate Rome's dominance. Military expeditions in Ethiopia and Arabia are mentioned. There were embassies from the kings of India, and special emphasis is given to Roman exploration of the western and northern coasts of Europe, including even an expedition to Jutland. Rome under Augustus was the first empire to reach these northern limits of the world. If Rome had not actually incorporated all these territories, she had at least shown that no power could seriously oppose her. The rhetoric stretched the facts to fit Rome's deeply cherished desire for world domination. We might recall what was said about the British Empire at the height of its pretensions, or some of the contemporary rhetoric of globalization.

The ends of the earth were important to the Roman religio-political ideology, and continued to be pursued after Augustus. The emperor Nero sent two centurions on an expedition to trace the source of the Nile, and they seem to have reached a point about nine degrees north of the Equator, not rediscovered by western explorers until 1839.[23] The Roman commander Agricola circumnavigated Britain in the 80s. The belief that Rome already dominated the οἰκουμένη even led to the idea of going beyond its edges, across the ocean, in search of new worlds to conquer, implementing, in effect, the plans that Alexander the Great had made, according to legend, and had only been prevented from achieving by his death. The Atlantic horizon especially beckoned, with *ultima Thule* as a symbol of the aspiration to conquer even the 'furthest' of islands.[24]

So when Luke describes Jesus' commission of his apostles as witness 'to the end of the world' (Acts 1:8) he evokes not only Isaianic prophecy (Isaiah 49:6, which

---

[23] Romm, *The Edges of the Earth in Ancient Thought*, pp. 155–6.
[24] Ibid., ch. 4.

accounts for the singular 'end') but surely also Roman political ideology. What Jesus projects is a counter-metanarrative, an alternative to Rome's, a narrative not of coercive power but of witness. Already by Acts 17:7, his disciples are being accused of turning the whole world (the οἰκουμένη) upside down. It may well be that in Luke 2, Luke already, with one of his always-understated hints of a Christian critique of empire, means to contrast the much-vaunted world domination of Caesar with the birth of the messianic king, ironically born a subject of Caesar. Roman power was inescapably religious: the state gods of Rome gave victory to the armies of Rome. So to witness to the kingdom of God as far as the edges of the earth, as Jesus commissioned his apostles to do, was to expose Rome's aspiration to limitless dominion as blasphemous.

Exactly this happens in the book of Revelation, not so completely different in this respect from Acts as is commonly supposed, but different, of course, in its stark anticipation of the way that faithful witness to God's kingdom will provoke violent suppression. Revelation echoes again and again the ideologically exaggerated claims of Roman power: all the inhabitants of the earth worship the beast and all nations drink from the cup of the whore of Babylon (Revelation 13:8; 18:3; cf. 17:2; 18:23). Rome with her divine pretensions and the true God contend for the allegiance of the nations, in a battle fought, on the one hand, with violence and deceit, and, on the other, by suffering witness to the truth, the witness Jesus and his followers bear. Notably, Rome is portrayed as a system not only of military violence and political tyranny (the beast of chapters 13 and 17), but also of economic exploitation (the harlot of Babylon in chapters 17 and 18). The harlot of Babylon, grown rich from her clients, is the city of Rome, 'the great city that rules over the kings of the earth' (17:18), whose vast consumption sucked in all the produce of the empire and all the trade, especially in luxury goods, that crossed the borders of the empire from distant lands to the east. In his representative and very accurate list of twenty-eight kinds of cargo shipped to Rome (18:12–13) and in his vivid portrait of the lamentations over Rome's fall by the specific categories of her subjects who profited from her trade – the merchants, ship-owners and sailors (18:9–20) – the prophet John shows himself quite attentive to the economic realities of his world. In this world system Rome was the centre growing rich through the impoverishment of her periphery. This is the nearest thing to contemporary economic globalization that we could reasonably expect from the first century of our era. John's list of the cargoes shipped to Rome ends emphatically with 'slaves – that is, human lives' (18:13, my translation): a comment on the whole list. It is in human lives that Rome trades. In view of the child slave labour that produces in some Asian countries the cheap goods wanted by the wealthy consumers of the west, the same comment on the contemporary globalized economy would surely be appropriate.

In Revelation those who bear the witness of Jesus, which is the witness to the truth of God's deity and kingdom, radically at odds with the world as the imperial power and its culture construct it, witness primarily by their sheer nonconformity. (This does not exclude any other form of witness, but it is the primary form of their witness.) By holding faithfully, even at the cost of their lives, to the truth of God and God's kingdom, by refusing to worship the beast or participate in Babylon's oppression, they falsify the beast's metanarrative with its claims to irresistible and universal power. They falsify the idolatrous claim that there is no alternative. The beast may seem to prove his supremacy in putting the witnesses to death, but in fact he proves that his power is no more than brute force and that the power of brute force has definite limits. He cannot compel their allegiance. He cannot eradicate their witness, since their deaths at the hands of the beast become themselves a powerful witness to the truth they refused to deny and to the Jesus whose own witness led to suffering and death. Witness to the truth, distinguished from the will to power by its willingness to suffer for the truth, confronts and defeats the will to power.

6. The biblical story and cultural diversity

The biblical story is apt to clash with the global meta-narratives of power, and, as we have seen in the case of 1 Corinthians, with local narratives that ape them. But this is not necessarily the case with all the local and individual narratives it encounters. The biblical story is not, as the narrative of economic globalization has been called, a cultural tidal wave sweeping away all the wonderful diversity of human culture.[25] Perhaps the miracle of tongues at Pentecost in Acts 2 is a symbol of this. It is a miracle that symbolically transcends the diversity of human languages: they no longer divide people or impede understanding, as they did at Babel. But this diversity of human languages is not abolished. Everyone hears the gospel in their own language. The miracle was in one sense quite superfluous, since virtually everyone there could have understood Greek, Aramaic or Latin. There was no practical need for such profligate speaking in all kinds of local languages. But God reverses Babel in such a way as rather conspicuously to affirm human

---

[25] Ellwood, *The No-Nonsense Guide to Globalization*, p. 53.

cultural diversity. When Paul states that in Christ there is no longer Jew, Greek, barbarian or Scythian (Colossians 3:11), what he denies is cultural privilege, not cultural diversity.

The biblical story is not only critical of other stories but also hospitable to other stories. On its way to the kingdom of God it does not abolish all other stories, but brings them all into relationship to itself and its way to the kingdom. It becomes the story of all stories, taking with it into the kingdom all that can be positively related to the God of Israel and Jesus. The presence of so many little stories within the biblical metanarrative, so many fragments and glimpses of other stories, within Scripture itself, is surely a sign and an earnest of that. The universal that is the kingdom of God is no dreary uniformity or oppressive denial of difference, but the milieu in which every particular reaches its true destiny in relation to the God who is the God of all because he is the God of Jesus. We may recall once more the Bible's final book, where Babylon, the ruler of the kings of the earth, comes to nothing, destroyed by its clash with the narrative of God's kingdom, but where also the nations bring their glory and honour into the new Jerusalem, that is, they bring all they have to offer as glory and praise given to God (Revelation 21:24–26).

7. Conclusion

Several Christian writers, reflecting on the complex phenomenon of contemporary globalization, have been reminded by it of what we have identified in this book as the biblical movement towards the universal. Peter Selby, for example, comments:

The range and speed with which it is now possible to engage with one another around the globe brings to the mind all that the Scriptures say about the global character of God's project, the universality of the divine ambition. It is hard not to feel the excitement of global communication as echoing in some sense the desire of a God for whom it is too light a thing to restore the exiles of Israel to their homeland, the triumphant conclusion of the Lucan narrative of the gospel's progress to the heart of the empire and the final cosmic glorification of the Lamb. God's purpose is global – in fact universal.[26]

Similarly, Bob Goudzwaard reflects:

[L]ong before the present process of technological and economic globalization began, God's message of global Good News went forth and began its work. The idea of globalization, therefore, is not foreign to the Bible ... [W]e might say that God's economy entails its own style of globalization, oriented to the coming of his Messiah King. The question, then, is not whether Christians should be for or against globalization. Instead, the question is, 'What kind of globalization should we be supporting?'[27]

What kind of globalization should we be supporting? The Christian church is uniquely placed in the contemporary world. In a world in which, more than ever before, global developments override both nation states and local communities, the Christian church is both an international movement and also essentially rooted in localities. Its God-given commission demands that it constantly cross boundaries, but only for the sake of those to whom

---

[26] Selby, 'The Silent Word Still Speaks', p. 100.
[27] B. Goudzwaard, *Globalization and the Kingdom of God* (Grand Rapids, Michigan: Baker, 2001), p. 20.

it comes in every particular place and context. Its mission distinguishes it from every force, political, economic or cultural, that works for the benefit of some at the expense of others. It cannot authentically exist as an imposition on others but only as people gladly make it their own. If it is to remain faithful to its Lord, it dare not let itself be co-opted by other interests and become the ideology of any of the other forces at work in this world.

Of course, the reality of the church has often been quite different, so often that the last paragraph will sound impossibly idealistic to many. But the church's mission is inseparable from continual repentance and constant heeding of God's call to God-given holiness, faithfulness and discernment. Contemporary globalization is a fresh situation in which these things must happen in an appropriately new way. Much that is happening by way of communication, understanding, participation and action across the boundaries of our world may be welcomed by Christians as having some real correspondence to 'God's own style of globalization' (Goudzwaard) or 'the global character of God's project, the universality of the divine ambition' (Selby). But much else must be exposed as the global ambition of forces of self-interest, exploitation and oppression that are directly opposed to God's concerns for the poor, the integrity and diversity of his creation, and the genuine flourishing of human life in community. This is a demanding situation of opportunity and challenge for Christian witness. It must send the church back to the Scriptures, outward in solidarity especially with the victims and the neglected, and forward in hope for the coming of the kingdom of God.